HOW TO WRITE A
COOKBOOK—AND SELL IT

HOW TO WRITE A
COOKBOOK–AND SELL IT

by Frances Sheridan Goulart

shley Books, Inc.
Port Washington, N. Y. 11050

HOW TO WRITE A COOKBOOK—AND SELL IT
© Copyright 1980 by Frances Sheridan Goulart.

Library of Congress Number: 80-13092
ISBN: 0-87949-180-9

ASHLEY BOOKS, INC./*Publishers*
Port Washington, New York 11050

Printed in the United States of America
First Edition

9 8 7 6 5 4 3 2 1

Library of Congress Cataloging in Publication Data:

GOULART, FRANCES SHERIDAN.
  How to write a cookbook—and sell it.

  Includes bibliographical references.

  1. Cookery—Authorship. I. Title.
TX644.G68   808'.025   80-13092
ISBN 0-87949-180-9

Contents

In the process of writing this book, I sent questionnaires to one hundred professional people—cookbook writers, and the people who edit, publish, agent, and sell cookbooks. Much of the information presented here would have been impossible without the kind cooperation of those who responded by phone, by mail, in person.

It is impossible to thank everyone by name. I hope therefore that this printed thank you will serve under the circumstances instead. One person who should not remain nameless, however, is my long-suffering typist. Special thanks to you, Esme Henry.

HOW TO WRITE A
COOKBOOK—AND SELL IT

Chapter I

The Joy of Cooking For Publication

"The publishers grind out more than three hundred a year ... and frankly we can't figure out who buys up all the stuff," say food writers Paula Wolfert and William Boyer.

Well, *we* can, because *we* do. We *all* do. Cookbooks are the literary equivalent of a box of candy. You can't stop after one. Maybe nobody should eat a whole box of candy. And nobody should own a whole room full of cookbooks either. But perfectly rational people do both.

Cookbooks are big business. And fortunately for you, too many cookbooks *don't* spoil the soup. They do, indeed, appear to enrich it.

Although 99 percent of all the cookbooks ever published are now out of print,* untranslated or otherwise un-

---

*To see some you've never even heard of, a trip to Radcliffe College's six-thousand-volume collection of cookbooks in its Schlesinger Library is a must.

available, five hundred new ones appear to take their place each year. Statistics tell us further that there are thirty-nine thousand new books published each year, five hundred of which—at a conservative estimate—are cookbooks. Moreover, three out of every ten women collect them, buying an average of three to five new titles each year, even though they already own at least thirty.

And while there are only two thousand cookbook titles in print, spare-no-expense collectors like Manhattan restauranteur and all-around epicure George Lang may number as many as four thousand volumes in his private collection alone.

And the boom extends well beyond books.

Cities like San Francisco, for instance, which could barely support ten cooking schools seven years ago, *today* boast more than one hundred. This pattern holds true throughout the country. There is hardly a home without a food processor and by 1984 it is estimated that 46 percent of all American homes will be using microwave ovens.

Cookware shops (with cooking schools inside them) are often operated by cookbook writers in their nonwriting hours. "A popular present [these days]," observes *House & Garden's* Penelope W. Linch, quoted in *Time* magazine (December 19, 1977), "is a cooking-school teacher's cookbook and a gift certificate for a series of lessons with the author."

Some of the other very hopeful signs insofar as the unpublished cook-cum-author is concerned were noted recently by a major news magazine: "There is a seemingly insatiable market for cookbooks. They are devoured and annotated in bed, at breakfast and on commuter trains." Noting that "the long term trend is generally toward more esoteric books on specialized foreign cuisines...[and] there has been a spate of books that adapt recipes to the new machines...[and] authors and publishers have rediscovered regional American cooking." But the fact is that cookbooks tend to repeat themselves.

According to Nancy and Dean Tudor's *Cooking For Entertaining,* an invaluable reference book for would-be cookbook writers,[11] Beyond the basic book there will be a similar but new cookbook to one that was issued four or five years ago...there will be a continuing interest and stream of cookbooks because the whole subject category turns over every five years or so." (page 10). A factor in your favor.

One of the first things to decide, therefore, is what kind of a book you have in mind, categorically speaking, and whether the market is bearish or bullish on the subject at present.

The next thing to decide is where your priorities lie. Says Ian Ballantine, founder of Ballantine Books, the first company in the country to publish paperback originals, "An author usually has a substantial reason for doing a book that has nothing to do with money."

Hopefully that applies to you. Because 99 percent of all publishers are "chintzy" but that very chintziness often works to your advantage (besides making you work harder, of course).

If your first priority is not to join the mighty who have risen but simply to get into print, you've got it made as long as your postage and patience hold out. There are, after all, twelve thousand book publishers and distributors in the United States.

If you are writing it down, and sending it out, and getting it back (maybe repeatedly), welcome to the club. Here at last are the answers and the solutions. Everything (hopefully) you've ever needed to know about writing and selling your own cookbook—from the kind of paper to type it on to the kind of bookstores and cookstores to promote it in—should appear somewhere in the chapters to follow.

If your manuscript is an immovable object, here's how to turn it into the money-making movable feast it was meant to be.

Chapter II

How a Cookbook Is Born

Part I: *Mastering The Art of French Cooking*

Fortunately for us all, there is no such animal as an "average" author or a "typical" cookbook. If there were, few of us would measure up.

It is comforting to know that no matter what your background, you're in the running.

Before he wrote his *Simple French Food*, voted best overall cookbook of 1974 and best foreign cookbook of the year, Richard Olney was an artist by trade. Bernard Clayton, Jr., who walked away with honors as the author of the year's outstanding "first" cookbook, *The Complete Book of Breads*, was a former war correspondent.

It is also comforting to know you are never too old—not just to begin, but to go on to best sellerdom.

Julia Child, for instance, didn't enroll in a cooking school until she was in her late thirties and it wasn't until 1961 when she was forty-nine that she finally published the first volume of her magnum opus, *Mastering The Art of French Cooking*. Her story should be an inspiration to us all, illustrating as it does how the course of a cookbook writer's career never runs smooth. It's more like lumpy gravy than true love.

When Julia enrolled at the Cordon Bleu*, her teachers were Max Bugnard, who had owned his own restaurant in Brussels before the war, Claude Thillmont, for many years the pastry chef at the Cafe de Paris, and Pierre Mangelatt, chef at an excellent small restaurant in Montmartre.

Bugnard, famed as a meat, vegetable and sauce cook, had known Escoffier. And Chef Thillmont had worked with Mme. Saint-Ange on her classic cookbook, *Le Livre de Cuisine de Mme. Saint-Ange*, in the 1920s. "Those two men knew just about everything there was to know," says Julia.

Julia's success as a television personality, of course, is a story all by itself. As for her first phenomenally successful cookbook? Oddly enough, the idea didn't even originate with Julia, "the one chef in the country who has the recog-

---

*The Cordon Bleau was founded in the nineteenth century and once served as a cooking school for orphans. By the 1930s, it had become a place where the affluent sent their staffs to learn the techniques of classic cookery. These days, to become a professional chef in France, you must serve as an apprentice for years in a restaurant or hotel kitchen, and that training is often supplemented by attendance at a government-sponsored technical institution, such as the Cordon Bleu school.

nition we are all striving for" as the Pacific Chefs Association has described her. Rather, as the story goes, a friend in Paris introduced her to Simone (Simca) Beck who had started to work with another friend of hers, Louisette Bertholle, on a book about French cooking for Americans. Through her new friends, Julia joined the Cercle des Gourmettes, a gastronomical society for women. The three took lessons here from a professional chef. Julia fell in love with the French "way" with food. But as for Simca's and Louisette's project? "I knew they needed an American collaborator—they'd had one who didn't work out for some reason," says Julia. "but I had no interest in it then. The book was their affair."

It wasn't, in fact, until 1951 (in the intervening years the three friends started a cooking school called, appropriately enough, the Ecole des Trois Gourmandes) that Julia made the book *her* affair as well.

The purpose of the book in Julia's mind was to overcome the American fear of elaborate French cuisine and to describe what a dish should look like and feel like at each stage in its preparation.

Creating such a serious, even semischolarly work took lots of time and research. But the first professional who read it knew Julia was "on to something" and passed the sample chapter and outline which Julia had prepared along to Houghton Miflin Company, a large publishing house in Boston.

The three authors were given a not very magnificent advance of $250 and a year to complete the book. According to the benefactor who brought Julia and Houghton Miffin together, Julia's samples left a lot to be desired. Julia was a rather poor writer at that point and her spelling was "atrocious." But "I could see," said the friend, "that this book...was really going to work."

Unfortunately, her publishers got considerably more than they bargained for and considerably less. Julia's eight-hundred-page typescript was turned in five years after her one-year deadline had come and gone.

The upshot was that the book was turned down apparently because of its length, its excessive detail, its overly academic tone.

The Childs moved to Oslo, Sweden, at this point and Julia spent the next year rewriting the entire book.

The second version covered more ground but seemed improved. Julia taught herself, with help from husband Paul and one or two other people, to write. But Houghton Mifflin again found it unpublishable. Koshland and Judith Jones, two Alfred Knopf editors interested in good food, read it and tried out some of the recipes. Judith Jones was immediately convinced that it was "revolutionary." It was, she says, "like having a teacher right there beside you in the kitchen."

Eventually the first volume of *Mastering the Art of French Cooking* came out in the fall of 1961, to virtually unanimous praise. Carig Claiborne called it "probably the most comprehensive, laudable, and monumental work on the subject," written "without compromise or condescension." The late Michael Field agreed. "It surpasses every other American book on French cooking," he said. James Beard, Dionne Lucas, and every major New York food writer concurred, and Houghton Mifflin has been regretting the one that got away ever since.

Part II: *The Quick And Easy Vegetarian Cook Book*

Not every cookbook writer has the Cordon Bleu in his background or Judith Jones in his foreground. Nor does every cookbook writer cook or write alone. Having a partner simplifies things. It cuts writing and recipe testing in half (even further if you have children between you), and it allows you to share expenses and the various physical as well as psychological burdens.

Ruth Ann and Bill Manners, authors of *The Quick and Easy Vegetarian Cookbook*, aren't married but they *are* family (brother and sister-in-law to be exact), and they are also vegetarians and enthusiastic cooks. Now at last they are also published writers of the same book.

Let their unlikely backgrounds be an inspiration to us all. Bill is a runner, a carpenter and a mystery writer most of the time. His sister-in-law (who lives, literally, a scone's throw away) has published books about sewing and home decoration. What they have in common is an intense interest in vegetarian cooking. (He's been a "meat-totaler" for fifty-five years, and she for three.) Their M. Evans book,

The Quick and Easy Vegetarian Cookbook, was published in hardcover in May of 1978 with a paperback (also M. Evans) issued in September, 1979.

"I had no idea of writing a book at first... until Ruth Ann became a convert," Bill says.

"Vegetarian dishes all seemed so complicated and time consuming at first until Bill shared his shortcuts with me," Ruth Ann remembers. "Eventually we both began to wonder if there might not be a market for a vegetarian cookbook that stressed ease and quickness. It didn't *seem* that anybody had done one."

It didn't seem that way to Bill's agent Roberta Pryor of International Creative Management (also by good chance a vegetarian) either, so she took on their proposal. This was not more than a few pages along (with no recipes at all), but its virtue seemed to be the convincing way it discussed the book's theme of ease and quickness for the person making a transition to a vegetarian diet.

The logical place to start it out was Knopf where Roberta had already sold Anna Thomas's highly successful *The Vegetarian Epicure*.

When Knopf editors didn't nibble at the carrot in front of their aggregate nose, Roberta went to Houghton Mifflin (another no), then to M. Evans and Company. Here, as good luck once again would have it, a vegetarian editor, Pamela Veley, read it. And liked it. And bought it—after asking for a half-dozen recipes which she tested herself and also liked.

"We sold it in April of 1977 and had it finished by September," Bill recalls. The Mannerses had the advantage of having two more-or-less vegetarian households available as tasters (Bill did half the recipes and Ruth Ann took the other). And, for the most part, they accepted one another's verdict on what did or did not succeed, gastronomically speaking.

If advance money, royalties and the contract in general were "fairly standard," the manner in which the Mannerses publicized themselves wasn't, largely thanks to the aggressive efforts of Ruth's husband, Dave, a professional public relations man.

Does it pay out of your own pocket to advertise yourself the way the Mannerses did—starting with local newspaper interviews and proceeding to radio and TV interviews as well in nearby and not-so-nearby cities like Boston, Philadelphia, Pittsburgh and Cleveland? (Impressed with their efforts close to home, Evans agreed to pay out-of-town expenses).

The two authors think so. "It got us the paperback sale," says Bill. Adds Ruth Ann, "In fact, it was mostly thanks to Dave's efforts that we made most of the appearances and did the cooking demonstrations."

And what did they learn from their experiences?

"There's no magic in it," says Ruth Ann. "Just lots of plain, hard, solid, hard work.

Mostly but not entirely. Hard work can produce its own magic.

For instance, how do you get your book into health food stores if your publisher hasn't done it for you?

You buy a couple hundred copies and go sell them yourself from door to door. It worked so well for Bill that the country's largest health-food book distributor, Nutri-Books, changed its tune and put in an order for five hundred copies when the paperback appeared.

If that isn't magic, it'll have to do until the real thing comes along.

Chapter III
Eating Your Own Words

"It's partly Julia Child, partly James Beard, and partly me" goes the caption on a 1975 *New Yorker* cartoon showing an oven-mitted wife serving a casserole to guests.

That's true of any recipe really, yours included. Only the names change. Some of your recipes may be one part Escoffier, one part Fannie Farmer and one part you, without your even knowing it! Since recipes don't come with names attached there is no way of protecting the innocent. In fact, there is no way of practicing innocence 100 percent of the time.

In other words, there is nothing new under the culinary sun. The first cookbook was reportedly written around 2000 B.C. by I. Ya of China. And no doubt it was barely off the presses before other cooks were helping themselves to what it had to offer. As far back as two thousand years ago, Pliny the Elder observed, "In comparing various authors with one another, I have discovered that some of the gravest and latest writers have transcribed, word for word, from former works, without making acknowledgement."

When it comes to what tangled webs we weave, nothing can compare with the intricacies of recipe "rights"— whether they are yours, mine, ours, or plain old public domain.

And there is plenty of plagiarism in the pantry. As James Beard politely puts it, "There are more typewriter cooks than real cooks out there."

Cookbook writer Karen Hess, who puts it even less politely, says, "Everyone steals recipes. It is not only tolerated, but is often encouraged by some editors and publishers who justify it by their claims that nobody invents a recipe anyway."

Well, who *does* that recipe you "adapted" from *Family Circle* legally belong to? And if you "borrow" Aunt Sophie's family formula for stroganoff and call it "Ukranian Beef Stew" in your book, can she sue you? And what if you "adapt" Julia Child's recipe for Boeuf Bourgignon— does a change of spices mean a change of ownership?

Can you go straight to jail without passing "go" or collecting your $500 advance if your editor gets sick on that recipe for rhubarb tonic where you called for the toxic leaves rather than the stalks (an honest mistake, you say)? Or says it sounds too much like Fannie Farmer?

The answer is probably not. But how can you avoid going to press with somebody else's Chicken Kiev on your conscience? The following suggestions and examples should help.

Don't worry excessively about lawsuits unless you are inept or dishonest. According to authors Paula Wolfert and William Boyer, "It seems that a recipe is considered an idea or a system, and an idea or a system cannot be protected by copyright. What *can* be protected is language, or rather a unique way to express an idea. Since illustrations for preparing food are not known for their artistry or wit, then, most probably, the expression of those recipes is not unique, and infringement, even on so massive a scale, could be difficult to prove."

Likewise, Judith B. Jones, a grand dame among cookbook editors (and an author as well) advises, "Of course, there's no really original recipe. Somebody has done it before. But you don't just copy it. You add your own touch, maybe just a different way of putting it together."

How does "fair use" pertain to recipes?

"Adapting,' a recipe gets you off the hook. But there's a fine line between theft and adaptation.

Here is a good example of the latter.

"Headlining the menu at all three restaurants—the Tree House and two called Good Ol' Days—is the flower pot sandwich, named for the bread that Sally bakes in the familiar red clay pots. 'I worked it out from an old Flemish recipe that called for two kinds of whole-wheat flour and pure honey,' Sally says. Patrons have a choice of six different fillings, including one she calls 'Happle'—a mixture of ham, apple and cheddar cheese. 'That recipe came from an old Pennsylvania Dutch cookbook.' "*

Make a clear statement in your proposal/manuscript of your intent. A book whose recipes are old, new, and *borrowed* as well as true-blue, is *American Food: The Gastronomic Story* by Evan Jones (Dutton). As he puts it, "the second half covers recipes...gathered from friends, restaurants and acquaintances all over the country, carefully chosen and tested by the author and his wife."

Be honest about where your nonoriginal work originated in order to safeguard yourself, your editor, your publisher and the reputation of your agent, if you have one. If your book is indeed a compilation of old family recipes or a new look at old favorites, just make sure that you give credit where credit is due. And even before making the acknowledgement, check back with your source and ask *how* the source would like to be credited.

Mel London, for instance, whose *Bread Winners* is a compilation of hundreds of *other* people's original recipes for breads, had every contributor sign a simple release form giving him permission to print the recipe with a credit line. You should do the same if you are doing such a collection.

Avoid (where possible) using recipes of uncertain origin. Avoid including recipes from friends and relatives no

---

*The cook is Sally Nichols in an interview in *Woman's Day, February 20, 1979.*

matter how ardently they vouch for their originality. Quite often the recipe has been "inadvertently" copied from a box, a magazine or a carton of noodles.

What happens when somebody is found guilty of "unofficial borrowings and recyclings," as one food writer has delicately put it?

It hurts the market for cookbook writers yet to come like yourself.

"I only buy books by people whose palates I know and trust," says food writer Jean Hewitt. "Recipe stealing is so rampant that if you get upset every time you see it you go nuts."

A good illustration of that sort of theft which Harper & Row editor Fran McCullough calls "scissors-and-paste-up jobs from back issues of *Gourmet*" comes from Pamela Harlech's *Feast Without Fuss*, a 1977 title from Atheneum.

At least one hundred and sixty-five recipes in the book appeared uncredited to either *Gourmet*, in whose pages they appeared, or to the well-known writers from whom they were filched, including Jane Grigson, Evan Jones, James Beard and others.

Testing, Testing

Almost as bad as the recipe that's not original is the recipe that's not tested.

"We worry about it all the time," says a Harper & Row

editor. "There's no way we can check but we *do* ask our authors questions."

In one sense a cookbook is like a book on home carpentry. The plans presented should work. Anyone who has invested $6.50 in the ingredients for a quiche Lorraine expects to get just that. And the only way you can be sure they will is to test your recipe, ideally more than once. Do not expect your editor to handle this. There may be many a slip between measuring cup and customer's lip, but it's better the slips occur in *your* kitchen rather than in that of the editor or the reader.

There is no "standard" procedure for testing but one way is to make a simple chart or form with lots of room for notes. You can try something like this:

TITLE: Chocolate cheesecake   *CHAPTER:* 3

SOURCE: Uncle Ed

TRIAL #2   DATE: August 7, 1980

                                  Method of
Ingredients: *Preparation:*
                                  1.
                                  2.
                                  3.
                                  4.

Comments: (Mine)

Comments: (Others)

Cost of Materials: *About 90 cents*

Remember as you test to keep track of your costs. And not for tax purposes alone. Most publishers are reasonable. Even if they refuse to finance their love affair with this book of yours they profess to love to the point of granting you an advance you can frequently get a token payment to help cover the costs of buying the food you need to properly test your recipes.

In fact, you may be able to get some help you probably didn't know was free for the asking.

Is your book about sugar or salt substitutes? Why not seek out the kitchen testing facilities of a firm in the business of marketing or manufacturing them, such as Adolph's. That's exactly what Helen Belinkie did when she wrote *Gourmet in the Low Calorie Kitchen* (David McKay, 1961).

Such a company might even consider putting in a good word for you and your project in the form of a brief preface or forward to accompany your proposal. It couldn't hurt to ask. And it would certainly do something for your credibility.

Is your book concerned with international cooking? Maybe a representative from a foreign consulate would provide you with an "endorsement." At the very least, you can utilize their research libraries.

When it comes to the actual testing, you should recruit outside mouths to help you. One's family is the first choice, but be prepared for rejection here, too.

The experiences of the co-authors of *The Quick and Easy Vegetarian Cookbook* are more typical than not. As Bill Manners explained to me, "Our kids were guinea pigs. We could count on them to tell us what they did, or didn't like. One recipe had to be tested seven times, but after the third round the response was loud and unanimous: 'What, *that* again?' " The children were also generous with instant, one-syllable judgments. A bread recipe, which one of Bill's daughters used to say was so good "it made you feel as though you were going to faint," is titled just that: "Faint." The not-so-good items, Bill reports, "were easily summed up with a simple 'Ick!' "

Another imaginative method of dealing with testing and its by-products is described by Helen Hecht and Linda LaBate Mushlin, authors of *Gifts In Good Taste:* "Dreaming up new ideas was, on the whole, easier than achieving a completely satisfactory result. We soon became eager volunteers for every school and community baked goods sale as outlets for our enthusiastic over-production. The bakery booth at our last school profited handsomely. Our freezers are presently overburdened with more recent experiments, and it requires strategic planning simply to open and close the freezer door. As we write this, we are impatiently awaiting the next fund-raising event."

In smaller publishing houses, editors themselves often function as testers or copy editors and proofreaders may take on the job. Which explains in Knopf's Judith Jones's opinion why there are "so many absolute disasters in this business."

On the other hand, the sixteen hundred recipes in a book like the *Betty Crocker Cookbook*, published by Golden Press in 1969, were tested for three years in the General Mills kitchens, then dispatched to one thousand three hundred homemaker-testers around the country.

The large women's service magazines such as *Parent's*, *Redbook* and *Better Homes and Gardens* operate like the large corporations. All have extravagant facilities and staffs for the extensive testing of recipes. If you sell a book to one of them, you can take advantage of such advantages.

Writing It Down

Now that you've perfected it in the pot, how do you put it on paper?

"Recipes," says food writer Anne Mendelson, "are a very imperfect way to teach anyone how to cook."

True. That's why they are so difficult to do properly. However, they *can* be done.

How about format? If you read enough cookbooks, you may understandably enough have the impression that just about anything goes, but it *doesn't*. It is best to steer clear of eccentric presentations. One example? Julia Child's twenty-two-page recipe for French bread in the second volume of *Mastering The Art Of French Cooking.*

One thing to avoid is what the author of *John Clancy's Fish Cookery* calls "lengthy, complicated recipes. Most people are frightened off by them."

Here is another example of bad form from a Chinese cookbook which should remain nameless (Wallace Yee Hong, *The Chinese Cookbook*, Crown, 1952):

STIR-FRY BITTER MELON WITH PORK
(Foo-Gar Chow Gee-Yoke)

A. 1 tablespoon peanut oil or lard
B. ¼ teaspoon salt
C. 2 cloves garlic
D. 1 tablespoon preserved black beans, crushed
E. ½ lb. fresh raw pork (tenderloin, butts, boned shoulder or side pork), cut in thin slices
F. 2 lbs. bitter melon (canned or fresh), cut in halves (seeds removed), and then cut in thin slices
G. 2 teaspoons light soy sauce
H. dash pepper
I. ½ teaspoon sugar
J. 1 teaspoon rice wine
K. 1 cup soup stock

L.   1 tablespoon cornstarch
M.   1 teaspoon seasoning powder

Preparation

Boil F about 3 minutes. Rinse in cold water and drain.
(Canned melon does not require boiling.) Mix together
G, H, I, J. Add 1 tablespoon water. Stir well when ready
to use. Mash C, D together in a separate bowl. Mix together L, M in a bowl with ½ cup water. Stir well when
ready to use.

Cooking

1. Put A in a large frying pan or skillet. Heat over high
   flame until almost smoking, then add B.
2. Add C, D preparation to the oil; fry ½ minute.
3. Add E. Stir-fry until pork is brown.
4. Add F. Stir-fry 2 minutes.
5. Add G, H, I, J preparation. Stir thoroughly.
6. Add K. Cover and cook 5 minutes.
7. Add L, M preparation and stir-fry until gravy thick-
   ens.
Serves 4.

Generally speaking, unless you have a very good reason

for using some other presentation, here are some rules of thumb for preparing recipes:

1. List each ingredient in the order in which it is used. Use standard measurements or market units, such as "one 16-ounce can tomatoes." Write the method as clearly as possible, making sure you say "stir" when that is the way the flour is mixed in or "beat" when appropriate. Give the pan sizes and specify the oven temperature for baking. Provide cooking times and doneness tests (springs back when the top is touched lightly with a finger, etc.). Give an estimated number of servings.

2. In working out recipes, write down every cupful, teaspoonful, or pinch of any ingredient. Use test sheets. Jot down the recipe with the date of the test. Make sure each ingredient is listed by its precise name.

3. A recipe with appeal reads as if it will taste good. Except for an occasional exotic recipe, time-tested food combinations are most appetizing in print.

4. A recipe must use ingredients generally obtainable where possible.

5. Use a minimum of ingredients without sacrificing quality.

One form universally accepted is the one used in *The New York Times*. You can see samples in any one of Craig Claiborne's books in any library.

Another format that is equally "readable" is this one from *Cooking With Michael Fields* (Holt, Rinehart and Winston, 1971.)

APPLE FRITTERS

In this recipe for deep-fried fruit in batter, which is Dutch in origin, the beer serves the same tenderizing functions as it does in the batter for shellfish. But because this batter contains no eggs, it produces a different type of coating. It is much like a crisp pastry, and it is dense enough to enclose the moist fruit securely.

These substantial fritters may be served as a dessert after a fairly simple main course, but they are equally effective accompanied by crisp bacon or a slice of grilled ham for breakfast or luncheon. Serves 4

The Batter:

1-3/4 cups sifted all-purpose flour
1½ cups beer (a 12-ounce can), preferably flat; if freshly opened, pour into a bowl and let it rest for 10 minutes or so to allow foam to subside

The Fruit:

½ cup granulated sugar
½ teaspoon cinnamon
4 medium apples, preferably Greenings (about 2 pounds), peeled, cored, and cut crosswise into ½-inch slices

For Frying:

Vegetable oil (or any vegetable shortening you prefer) to fill your deep fryer to a depth of at least 3 inches
For Dusting the Fritters:
Confectioners' sugar

Making the batter. Pour the sifted flour into a 2-quart mixing bowl and add the beer. Then, using a wire whisk, stir—don't beat—the two together for about 2 minutes, or until the mixture is quite smooth. The batter may be used at once, but it will have a far better texture if it is allowed to rest, uncovered and at room temperature for 2 hours.
Preparing the fruit. In a small bowl, mix together the granulated sugar and the cinnamon. Dip each slice of apple into the mixture, coating both sides. Place the slices on a cake rack set over a sheet of wax paper and let them rest for 30 minutes, but no longer.

Line a shallow pan with a double layer of paper towels.

Just before you fry the fritters, preheat your oven at its lowest setting and place a serving platter and the plates in it to warm.
Deep Frying the fritters: Heat the fat in your frying kettle or electric deep fryer to 375° F. If your fryer has a basket, set it in place to preheat. Then quickly proceed to coat and deep fry the apples.

Set the bowl of batter and the rack of apple slices close to the deep fryer. With tongs, pick up a slice of apple, dip it into the batter, then hold it above the bowl to allow the excess batter to drain off. Gently drop it into the hot fat.

Repeat this procedure rapidly with 3 or 4 more slices; remember not to overcrowd the frying kettle. Let the fritters fry undisturbed for a minute or two, then turn them carefully with tongs. As they continue to fry, turn the fritters every minute or so until they are golden brown and crusty. They should take about 5 minutes in all to cook through.

Remove the finished fritters from the pot with tongs and drain them on the paper-lined pan. Gently pat them with more paper towels to remove any excess fat. Set the pan in the preheated oven. Then quickly fry and drain the remaining apple slices in batches of the same size as the first one.

Chapter IV

Preparing The Proposal and Manuscript

"A man who is careful with his palate is not likely to be careless with his paragraphs," observed writer and epicure Clifton Fadiman.

Maybe. Still, writing a book about the beer and skittles nobody is better at than you isn't all beer and skittles.

First of all, get organized. Good work habits may not be everything, but they stand for a whole lot more than you may think.

Good work habits like a logically ordered kitchen are indispensable in turning out a good product.

"She's the most organized person I've ever met," says a friend of Julia Child. "Her library of books on food and cooking and her extensive files of material on the subject are arranged and cross-referenced with the care and thoroughness of a major research institute...she can afford to appear casual because she knows precisely what she is doing," says the *New Yorker* writer Calvin Tompkins. You should, too.

Editors look for other qualities besides good ideas and yummy recipes.

"Clarity and legibility" is what the publisher of the vegetarian cookbook *Wings of Life* said he likes to see in a manuscript.

"The cleaner the better," agrees the president of Minnesota's Meadowbrook Press. "This communicates that the author has a professional attitude about the whole process of getting published... it communicates that it would be easier to receive a timely, quality work from that author."

The recipes are the easy part, or as one veteran cookbook editor puts it, "A bunch of recipes does not a cookbook make... it takes expertise to produce a saleable cookbook."

Your choices boil down to two: to write the entire manuscript (plus a "query" letter to discover who wants to see it) or to write a proposal (book outline) which is a preview of the book to come.

Since an editor who wants to buy your book will have definite ideas about how the finished manuscript should look, you are better off writing a proposal. But the guidelines that follow apply to manuscripts, too, only more so.

1. How long (or short) should your proposal be? That depends. If you shine at short-windedness, you may be able to sum up your book nicely in five pages of prose and

an additional ten pages of recipes. If you are the patient, deliberative type, you may be more comfortable with twenty pages of text and forty pages of recipes.

2. Quantity takes a back seat to quality every time. As cookbook author Jeanne Voltz puts it, "The purpose of a proposal is to tempt the editor to part with money for your proposed manuscript and to give a clue to your writing ability."

Ask yourself several times while you're working and when you've finished whether you've met this objective.

More specifically, Voltz advises, "A proposal for an article or a book should explain briefly but clearly the main idea of your work: *Mama's Best Recipes for Today's Busy People, How to Entertain on a Budget, or Everything You Wanted to Know about Tomatoes—But Didn't Know Whom to Ask* ... and ... express your enthusiasm for the subject, how you will develop it, and how you amassed this knowledge of mama's recipes gone modern, budget entertaining, or tomato enjoyment. Then list the recipes with brief descriptions that you plan to use. Also, list your credentials. Publishers by necessity consider an author's sales potential, which can include a recognizable name or writing credits. Any published articles should be listed ... also include your evaluation of who will buy the book and why it is timely.

You'll have a lot of explaining to do in your first proposal. Like your first child, it's something you'll probably want to spend some time on. After that, you'll need fewer pages and less time to say what you have to say to sell it on future proposals.

That's how it was for Mel London who is now at work on his third cookbook for Rodale Press. "The first proposal," says London who also advises against turning in unsolicited and completed manuscripts, "was fifty-eight pages long, the second was eighteen pages, and the last one I sold with a phone call."

3. *How to Submit Your Proposal/Manuscript*

A. Type it neatly or have a manuscript typist do it. Typists usually charge by the page and the cost varies in different areas of the country. Edit carefully before typing. Your name and address should appear at the top left corner of the first page. Single recipes should have name and address at the top of the page. Manuscripts are always double or triple spaced to allow room for editing.

B. Keep two carbon copies. (Manuscripts have been lost.) Don't submit a photocopy or carbon unless you mention that you are submitting a copy to safeguard against loss of the original. (Editors may suspect that you are guilty of multiple submissions if you send a copy.) Because a proposal will always be read by more than one editor in a house, it's not a bad idea to send two copies—the original and a good sharp copy—so that two people can conceivably read simultaneously. (If nothing else, it saves you the trouble of re-sending the copy should your original disappear.) Your proposal should be addressed specifically; to The Editorial Department or The Editors—Cookbooks. Check a recent copy of *Literary Market Place* or *Writer's Market* for editors' names. Or check the indexes of *The Writer* and *Writer's Digest* to see if they've done this type of listing within the last six months.

C. Staple your proposal together or enclose it in a folder. A book manuscript should be mailed in a box (a typing paper box, for instance). The pages should be put into the box loose, *without* clips or staples.

D. Book manuscripts may be sent by first-class mail or, less expensively, by special fourth-class manuscript rate. Envelopes and packages must be marked Special Fourth-Class Rate—Manuscript on the outside. (Be sure stamped return envelopes are also marked Special Fourth Rate—Manuscript. You may insure manuscripts marked this way and secure a receipt at the post office. Manuscripts may be insured up to $200; for rates, inquire at your post office.)

E. Letters may *not* be enclosed with manuscripts at the above manuscript postage rates. If you wish to include a letter you may do so, provided you state on the outside of the package that first-class material is enclosed, and place additional first-class postage on the package.

F. Do not fail to enclose the *correct* amount of return postage when submitting a manuscript. Indicate the type of return mail to be used, such as Special Fourth-Class Rate—Manuscript, and give special instructions if you wish to have the manuscript insured.

4. *The Cover Letter* accompanies your proposal or manuscript.

While perhaps the best advice where your proposal is concerned is "over-say," the opposite is true of your cover letter. A note quickly explaining what you are sending and why is all that is called for.

For example:

> Dear (Editor's Name):
> If anyone knows a good cookbook idea whose idea has come, it is you.
> So I hope you will see the same promise in my enclosed proposal that I do.
> Thank you for your consideration.
>
> > Sincerely yours,
> > name
> > address
> > phone no.
>
> Encl: proposal (10 pages)
> > SASE

5. A proposal and mauscript, like any story, must have a beginning, a middle, and an end. There are no written rules, but there *are* guidelines. For instance, you must provide (in this order):

A. Title Page (do not number).

B. Author's Biography.

C. About This Book: one-page synopsis of what you will cover; number of pages, charts, etc.; number of recipes; and length of time the work will require on your part.

D. About The Market: a brief assessment of the market that you think exists for your book.

E. *Front Matter: Introduction, preface, foreward (not all are necessary).

F. Table of Contents.

G. The Recipe Index: a listing of as many of the recipes to appear as possible.

H. The Recipes: a dozen completed samples for the proposal or, at most, two dozen.

I. Back Matter: Appendix including sources, recommended reading, bibliography, etc. and Index.

Sample Authors' Biographies

(example #1)

ELLEN SUE SPIVACK
606 Market Street
Lewisburg, Pa. 17837
717-523-3277 or 3278

---

*Manuscript only would contain these. Proposal simply notes them on the Table of Contents page.

CAREER EXPERIENCE

Freelance Writer for health-oriented publications, regularly in *Well-Being, Vegetarian Times,* and *Bestways,* as well as Food editor for *Vegetarian World,* 1976-1977. Articles also sold to *Woman's Day, Bike World,* and *Mother Earth News.* Weekly column called Kitchen Nutrition has been appearing in the Union County *Journal* for four years.

Founder and Co-Operator of Lewisburg's natural food store, Deep Roots Trading Company. As part of store service, I give food demonstrations, lectures, and natural foods cooking classes. Focus a great deal of attention on supplying nutritional information to customers through books, periodicals, and information gleaned from health clinics and physicians who practice natural healing.

Author and Publisher of cookbook entitled *Beginner's Guide to Meatless Casseroles,* based on cooking classes.

Teacher of natural foods and vegetarian lifestyle classes within Bucknell University's mini-course program.

Lecturer/Demonstrator at North American Vegetarian Congress, 1978.

EDUCATION

Douglass College, New Brunswick, N.J. 1955-1959. B.S. in Education and Sociology. Named to Dean's List and graduated in top 10% of class.

Hamilton High School, Trenton, N.J. 1951-1955. Editor of yearbook. Graduated co-valedictorian with three college scholarships.

OTHER INFORMATION
Married with 3 children, 14 and 15½ years of age, 6 months. References furnished on request.

(example #2)
Frances Sheridan Goulart
232 Georgetown Rd.
Weston, Connecticut 06883
(203) 227-1587

ABOUT THE AUTHOR
"Frances Sheridan Goulart," says the best-seller *The Complete Book of Running* "is a vegetarian athlete...a racer as well as a runner...and a remarkable woman."

She is also the forty-two-year-old Detroit-born amateur athlete and author of *Eating To Win: Food Psyching For The Athlete* which investigates the link between sports and nutrition (Stein and Day, 1978) and four natural-foods-oriented cookbooks including *Bone Appetit: Natural Pet-food Recipes* (Pacific Search, 1976); *Bum Steers: The Meat Substitute Cookbook* (Chatham Press, 1975); and *The Mother Goose Cookbook* (Price/Stern/Sloan, 1970). Her newest cookbook, *20 Carrots: The Vegetarian Weight Loss Cookbook*, will be published in 1980.

Ms. Goulart is the founder and director of the Potsan-jammer School of Natural Cooking of Fairfield County.

Her articles on health, cooking, and nutrition and sports have appeared in *Women Sports*, *The New York Times*, *The New York News*, *Vogue*, *United Features Syndicate Newspapers*, *Vegetarian Times*, *The Herbalist*, *Bike World*, and she writes regularly for all three of the country's racquetball magazines, as well as the official journal of the Handball Association of America, and *The Jogger*, the official publication of the International Jogging Association of America.

In her spare hours, Ms. Goulart is one of Connecticut's top female long-distance runners with many titles and trophies to her credit.

She is also a swimmer and cyclist, covering more than 4,000 miles a year, and is a member of the Sound Cyclists Bicycle Club and the League of American Wheelman. She won her first bike marathon in 1978 in Weston, Conn.

In private life she is wife of science-fiction writer Ron Goulart. They live with their two sons in Weston, Conn.

6. *The Query Letter* is a proposal in digest form. It presents your idea in a few well-chosen paragraphs. If you have a complete manuscript or a long proposal in your "out" box, it's beter to hold your fire until you get a positive response to the idea from some editor.

Here are two samples. There is no "standard,' but remember the point is to make your point in a page or less.

(example # 1)
606 Market Street
Lewisburg, Pa. 17837
May 17, 1979

Fawcett Publishers, Inc./Gold Medal Books
1515 Broadway
New York, N.Y. 10036
Gentlemen:

I am very excited about my new book, *Good Food for Kids: A Natural Foods Guide for Bewildered Parents*. It focuses on the kitchen, the supermarket, and the natural foods store, where many parents are wrestling with the problems of proper food for their school-age children.

In our own natural foods store I am constantly confronted by these same parents seeking better food alternatives and nutritional information for their children's diet, but bewildered about where to start or how to proceed. They are seeking a practical, useful, and supportive approach to these problems.

Other new books in this area, which are generally written by doctors or nutritionists, deal with the subject of diet and its relationship to health from a technical viewpoint. In contrast, my book is *not* technical; it is "kitchen nutrition." It tackles food problems with relevant topics and hints, as well as with simple, kitchen-tested whole food recipes and menu ideas written in everyday language. *Good Food for Kids* is more than a cookbook; it is a whole foods book that I sincerely believe fills a how-to-start gap for a growing number of concerned parents.

I would like to send you a sample chapter. Using my outline below, please indicate which chapter you would like to see. Enclosed is an addressed postcard for this purpose. I am looking forward to hearing from you.

Outline for *Good Food for Kids: A Natural Foods Guide For Bewildered Parents* by Ellen Sue Spivack, copyright 1979.

Chapter 1   Back to Basics
Chapter 2   Getting Started
Chapter 3   Changing to Good Foods: The Kitchen in Transition
Chapter 4   Good Food on a Budget
Chapter 5   A Tour Through a Natural Foods Store
Chapter 6   Essential Utensils of a Good Foods Kitchen
Chapter 7   Meal Planning
Chapter 8   Snackin' on Good Food
Chapter 9   Good Food for Special Problems
Chapter 10 Good Food Recipes

Bibliography
Resource List
Glossary
Brand Name List
Recipe Index

Resume enclosed   Sincerely,
                                   Ellen Sue Spivack

(example #2)

Here is how Helen Hecht and Linda LaBate Mushlin described what became their book *Gifts in Good Taste* (Atheneum, 1979):

> The idea for these recipes evolved because we had been in the habit of regularly sharing some innovation from our kitchens with one another, and we observed more and more of our friends giving gifts of food they had made themselves. We felt a need for a collection of special recipes for giving on a variety of occasions. And since we both spend more time in the Kitchen than we can rationally account for, this project seemed a logical and welcome enterprise.

Clearly, simply and briefly put.

This statement of purpose would be followed by another paragraph listing the types of recipes and foods to be included. A third and final paragraph would sum up the authors' backgrounds.

SPECIAL NOTES
"About The Market For This Book" (Section C above)

A small publisher, because of this very smallness, is more interested in this section than his larger colleagues who have funds and in-house resources for carrying out their own market research. A small house is likely to be staffed with people who double as editors and production people or copy editors-cum-production people.

Unfortunately, the market research section is also often the toughest part of the outline for you to do because it is only peripherally related to the subject you know best: food.

Nevertheless, if you are serious about selling your book, you must give the publisher as many reasons as you can why you think your book will sell. There has to be a point of difference, even if it is only a slight one, between *your* book and the books that are already around. There must be something that gives the editor what's known in advertising as "a reason to buy."

For instance, why did Holt, Rinehart publish *John Clancy's Fish Cookery* when there were already numerous volumes on the subject available? Perhaps the selling point was, as *New York Daily News* reporter Suzanne Hamlin observed (October 31, 1979), "It is a teaching book, a cooking course within covers."

If that's true of your book, say so.

Or consider *Cooking with a Harvard Accent*, written by Melanie Marcus and published by Houghton Mifflin. *"Cooking with a Harvard Accent* . . . gives us a sampling of recipes from Harvard faculty and students past and present, with delightful introductions to both the cook and the contribution. The menu runs from hors d'oeuvres to dessert, and virtually every country and culture is represented in her introduction, though, the author, who once worked on the school's alumni magazine, admits that she rejected one recipe for 'Screaming Hawaiian Meatballs' that began: 'Take off all your clothes and roll around in 15 pounds of hamburger meat...' The ones she includes—Iroquois Roast Corn Soup, say, or Ted Kennedy's Beef Stroganoff—will provide unusual and welcome additions to any cook's repertoire." (*People* January 21, 1980, page 12.)

And it couldn't hurt to throw in facts and figures from the marketplace at your editor-to-be who, if he is like most editors, hasn't done all his homework. Does he know that "The primitive reason that so many cookbooks are published," according to Marcia Seligson, a reporter for *The New York Times* "is that they all sell?"

And is your editor aware that, according to one highly placed sales executive at New American Library, "It's an amazing market.

Practically every cookbook published will make a profit. And it just seems to be mushrooming every year." Does he know that three out of ten women buy books and that they buy three or more new ones each year on an average?

If you read the "trade" journals—and you should (see Books For Cooks in the Appendix)—and the writer's magazines and annuals, you will discover many more amazing facts to utilize as sales tools.

What else should you or could you include? While a cover letter is a must and a query letter is a maybe, an endorsement in the form of a foreward to your book definitely carries clout, especially if it comes from an authority or expert in the special area you are writing about. It can be as brief as a sentence or two.

Do not include artwork or photography. It is customary for the publisher to locate the artist and/or photographer who will provide cover art and inside illustrations after the final manuscript has been delivered and proofed. Exceptions? If you are a professional artist (or photographer), by all means include samples of how you would illustrate the book, if you do indeed wish to handle that job, too.

Remember that any material called for in your book other than text will just up the cost of producing it and decrease the chance of your selling it. You can price yourself right out of the running by indicating that expensive artwork, photography or lettering is essential to the life of your cookbook. Concentrate on the idea, or expressing it tersely and winningly. Leave the fancy footwork for later and to somebody else.

Preparing a Finished Manuscript

Some things are inevitable like death, taxes and the certainty that something will go wrong if you type your own manuscript yourself.

The expenses of typing your book and indexing it are yours to bear. Still this is no place to cut corners. If you insist on submitting a finished manuscript rather than a proposal (or when the time comes to get your manuscript completely typed), you would be well advised to farm it out to a competent manuscript typist. If you don't know one, call up the nearest publisher and ask any editor. Or get a recommendation from your local newspaper or simply look in the classified ads or phone directory under "business services."

Another "detail" job similar to typing that is worth delegating is the preparation of your index. Cookbook writers are divided into two camps: those who do it themselves and those who don't.

"The book should be well indexed," says the Bowker reference book *Cooking For Entertaining*, "by main ingredient and by important minor ingredients. There should be adequate cross-references from regional names, foreign or national names, unique title of dish, type of course or dish, perhaps season of serving, peculiar or unique preparation methods, and so forth."

Sounds like a big job? It is. It may cost you a couple of hundred dollars to have done, but this expense can be subtracted later from your first royalty check.

Chapter V

The 10 Percent Solution: Getting An Agent

Having whipped your kitchen chronicles, or at least your outline or the idea for them, into shape, the next step is getting an agent. Or is it? Does it pay to have one or will it wind up costing you more than it's worth?

Opinion is divided, to say the least.

First, the good news...

1. "Some writers are so demoralized by a rejection that they can't work for weeks, or they want to burn their manuscripts," says Lea Braff who represented such cookbook names as Elizabeth Ortiz-Lambert and Louise Brunner during her apprenticeship with the Julian Bach Agency. "An agent acts as a buffer and provides ongoing support."

2. "Editors *want* writers to have agents," says agent Lynn Nesbitt, a luminary with ICM, one of the country's largest agencies and a representative for several

top-money cookbook authors. "They want the writer to have a business representative. There is less chance then of a writer being disappointed with the contract, production and distribution."

3. Author Mary Louise Lau (*The Delicious World of Raw Foods,* (published by Rawson Wade, Emmaus, Pennsylvania) calls *her* agent, Knox Burger, "formidable." And the two authors of *The Prudent Diet* don't think they could have done it without *their* agent, Carmen Gomenplaz. Likewise, the energetic author of *Bread winners* thinks not having an agnet is like going through winter without an overcoat. "The competition out there is tremendous...most people simply don't know enough to deal with publishers. .."

4. "What's the best advice I could give a beginning cookbook writer?" asks Joanne Hush. "Get an agent."*

And then the bad news...

1. Surprisingly enough, even agents view their powers as less miraculous than the writers who turn to them. "Does having an agent improve the unpublished writer's chances? Probably not," says Lea Braff. "Agents are most useful in negotiations."

----

*If you want to get *her* agent, he's Robert Lescher.

Another agent (name withheld) was considerably less self-effacing. "If the author is smart enough to listen, I can save his life."

But Stein and Day's senior editor, Benton Arnovitz, thinks the help is likelier to be only marginal.

Before you leap from your own private frying pan into any partnership, consider what (ideally) an agent can do for you:

A. Seek the publisher best suited to your work. An agent keeps up with each publisher's recent books, so would know, for example, that a certain publisher has a new fish cookery cookbook and would not be interested in another.
B. Help you get the best contract and advance.
C. Advise you on the strengths and weaknesses of publishers who make offers on your manuscript. For instance, the agent knows which publishers provide strongest sales support.
D. Suggest how you can make your book or article more salable.

"Basically," says agent Bobbie Siegel, "it is in the area of contract negotiation that an agent can best help an author. You can give too much away by doing your own negotiating."

2. Agented or agentless, you must be a constant and persistent sleuth. Markets come and go and you can-

not let your agent's fingers do *all* the walking. A new publishing venture that is doing well with *one* cook-book, for instance, may well be in a receptive mood for a successor, your cookbook-to-be, for instance. You may read about new publishers anywhere and you may spot an opportunity before your busy agent does. For instance, Fawcett Books is starting a new line of large-format paperbacks called Columbine Books, Senior Editor Olga Vezeris recently told us. I also read the announcement in *The Writer* (January, 1980): "We are aiming at a mass-market audience and want *non-fiction of a highly salable nature..*
. We're actively looking for books on a variety of *self-help topics*, and will consider cookbooks" (my Italics).

3. Since the second most frequent reason writers part company with their representatives is "disagreement over the quality and salability of a potential book," according to a survey by the Book Industry Study Group, it is imperative that you pick an agent who sees in your work what you do and the markets for it that you do. Many agents refuse to submit a property to "minor league" markets. Why? Because an agent lives on his 10 percent commission and must deal only with the major markets. It's simply not worth any agent's while to send your manuscript or pro-posal to the small presses with limited funds.

Agents

"I find that most agents I've dealt with haven't been on target in terms of understanding the kind of thing we're doing...and...I haven't seen any evidence of superior proposal letter writing from agents," says best-selling cookbook writer and editor Vicki Lansky, whose "minor league" publishing house entered the semi-majors almost overnight on the strength of a single cookbook.

Some agents—usually those who are smaller or newer—don't operate that way.

Here, for example, is a who's who of publishers agent Lea Braff thought might like to see one of her client's proposals for a vegetarian weight-loss cookbook.

As she explained in a letter to the author, "I would like to hit three categories of publishers: the established cookbook publishers; the ones who may not specialize in cookbooks, but who do know your work; and the smaller, sometimes quite good publishers who specialize in healthy lifestyle books.

"My thinking now comes down to:

I.	II.	III.
Random House	Fawcett	Running Press
Simon and Schuster	Stein & Day	101 Productions
	Everest House	Strawberry Hill Press
St. Martin's	Chatham House	Stackpole
Thomas Nelson	Pacific Search Books	Acropolis Books
Doubleday	Grosset	Stephen Greene
Atheneum	Macmillan	Fresh Press
G.P. Putnam's	Barron's (*last*)	Ross Books"

Many agents, however, like Candida Donadio (who at one time had a client roster of two hundred) are "selective."

"If I take on a writer, I can usually sell his work within three submissions," she says.

In other words, the fourth time at bat you may find yourself all alone.

Not atypical is the experience of Lewisburg, Pennsylvania's Ellen Sue Spivack, author of *Meatless Casseroles*: "I had an agent but he did nothing. So now I am my *own* agent, but I *would* turn my work over to a good agent if I found one."

That of course is the trick.

A good agent, like a good man, is hard to find. You could wind up with the *other* kind, the kind who charges for his services before any deal has been consummated.

Another good reason *not* to get an agent until you're ready is that even an agent can't work monetary miracles for you if you are unpublished. Put another way, by publisher Howard B. Weeks, "The extent to which the author can make demands depends on the author's relative standing and bargaining position."

Some authors bargain better than their agents anyway. This brings up another problem with being bound to an intermediary. One of you will have to be the better half of the relationship and if your agent is any good, it won't be you. And if he isn't, you don't need him.

But if you decide not to be among the have-nots, agentwise, how do you get one? In the opinion of *Literary Mar-*

ket Place (another trade "bible" which is issued yearly). there are about eighty-five reputable agents to pick from. And a number of them like Virginia Barber, Julian Bach and Scott Meredith number successful cookbook authors among their clients. Some agents "agent" badly, some do it well. Which is which?

Unfortunately, client lists are generally for the scrutiny of editors alone and otherwise are kept confidential. Agent Virginia Barber suggests, 'It is better to ask what *kind* of clients an agent represents, rather than clients' *names.*" You can do this either by a letter or phone call. Or you can have an agent personally recommended to you (or vice versa).

The Society of Author's Representatives explains why. "If it were known that such and such an agent represented a lot of children's books, that agent would inevitably be deluged by every piece of doggerel, ostensibly written for kids."

And what's true of kids' books is true of cookbooks.

Where are Lists of Agents Found?

1. *Literary Market Place* (R.R. Bowker Co.), annual directory of the book publishing trade, lists more than one hundred and fifty agents and agencies in New York City, California, and elsewhere. Reference rooms in most libraries have copies. (Address in Appendix 4.)

2. *The Society of Authors' Representatives* (SAR), a voluntary association of New York City literary and dramatic agents, publishes a pamphlet entitled *The Literary Agent*

with the names and addresses of its members. (Address in Appendix 4.)

3. *Independent Literary Agents Association, Inc.* (ILAA), a new voluntary association of literary and dramatic agents, will send a list of its members upon request. Write to: Independent Literary Agents Association, Inc., c/o Phyllis Seidel, Phyllis Seidel Literary Agency, 164 East 93rd St., New York, N.Y. 10028.

4. Poets and Writers (201 West 54th Street, New York, N.Y. 10019) publishes *Literary Agents: A Complete Guide* for $2.50.

5. See "Agents: literary" in the yellow pages of the Manhattan Telephone Directory.

Judith Appelbaum, managing editor of *Publishers Weekly*, suggests you locate an agent by having one recommended to you by another local writer (go to readings, conferences or workshops), a local writer's club, or one of the libraries in your area. Or perhaps even better, "when you finally find an editor who expresses interest in your book, ask *him* to suggest a good agent."

Also be sure you know your friends from your enemies. There are large agencies, small agencies and agencies that advertise and charge fees for handling, reading and criticizing your manuscript. This may happen in person or by mail with fees ranging from ten dollars up.

The latter group of agents is generally regarded with suspicion. And with good reason.

"The editorial help usually comes with a heady dose of flattery and crocodile tears over publisher rejections," advises one guide to literary agents. "Some fee-charging agents may accept a fee in advance and then hold the manuscript for months before giving the promised service. (Withholding any prepaid service longer than three months is illegal unless the customer is allowed to cancel the order and get a refund. An agent who breaks this law can be sued by a writer)...or...Some fee-charging agents may submit a manuscript to a publisher who will then try to get several thousand dollars from the author for subsidized publication."

Let the writer beware.

Recipe for a Successful Contract: Ante-ing up

Paltry is the name of the game when it comes to "money in front," otherwise known as an author's advance.

Even Julia Child had to split her less than paltry advance of $250 with her two collaborators for *Mastering The Art of French Cooking* which the publisher, Houghton Mifflin as it happens, subsequently turned down anyway, not once but twice.

The truth of the matter is that the less you're willing to take, the better your chances of getting your cookbook published somewhere by someone.

There is no better way to spend your time while waiting for letters or returned proposals than to educate yourself in the realities of writing. "Front" money, for instance.

Cookbook Advances

For every Paula Wolfert, who thinks that "an advance of $5,000 would not be too generous for a beginning writer to expect," there are ten writers with ten books to their credit who would like to know how she got it.

Herb writers Connie and Arnold Krochmal, for instance, say "no advance" would be a more reasonable expectation.

Asked how generous an advance a beginning cookbook writer might expect, Judith Applebaum, managing editor of *Publishers Weekly* replied, "That depends on the book and the author."

Benton Arnovitz, Stein and Day senior editor, spoke for many fellow editors when he replied, "Modest unless the author has a big name in the field."

Agent Lea Braff, however, did not mince words. "Small" was her prediction, but like many of her partners in publishing, she cautioned that it would be a mistake for the beginning writer "to share the publisher's risk, or work for a royalty alone."

The median advance for books published in fall winter 1975-76, says an Authors' Guild survey, is $5,000. But median doesn't mean much except to the writers who get it. Because even publishers who *can* pay reasonable advances don't. "You can expect zero to $2,000, but some of the best cookbook publishers," grumbles a well-known author who chose to remain nameless, "don't pay any."

Indeed, says Pennsylvania-based writer Ellen Spivack, who was the publisher of her own mail-order cookbook *Meatless Casseroles* and is now seeking out somebody else to handle the chores for her second, *Good Food for Kids,* "You can expect about $1,000 to insure that the publisher will push the book and the writer will make a sincere effort to meet the publisher's need for corrections, etc," but she admits that the only solid offer she's had, out of the fifty publishers queried on her second project, was a contract but no advance.

A lot depends on who you are and how many copies the publisher thinks he can sell.

So don't count your advances before they're hatched. As cookbook writer Jeanne Voltz cautions:

> An advance for a contract drawn on the basis of the proposal provides money while you work, but not all beginners can bring off such a windfall, with or without an agent. And don't expect the million-dollar—or even $100,000—advances that you read about in gossip columns. Those are few, so few that they're good gossip. The advance is against royalties, so you won't get additional money until the advance has been recovered. Figure how many copies of a book must be sold before you, the author, make back $100,000, at 10 percent on the first five thousand copies, 12½ percent on subsequent copies, if the book is priced at $12.95.

But even if it's less than you'd like, maybe you ought to take the money and run because it is one step of the way toward turning you into a professional, which is what you want to be, because it's what makes writing easier and the money that goes with it easier to get.

"I'd be willing to trade advance money or royalty points to sign with the best publisher for the book," says Vicki Lansky, an example of that unique animal, the writer who also edits and publishes. "The author should make the best deal he or she can...but the book must be profitable to the publisher or there won't be a second chance."

Actually, there are things money can't buy. Before you rule out the no-money in front (no advance) houses, consider what services they provide that a major house might not.

Distribution to Stores, Libraries, and Mail-Order Sales

After all, people can't buy a book they can't find or haven't heard about.

1. Find out if the house considering you has its own sales force. And if so, how well and how often it covers its territories.

2. You might want to turn thumbs down if they depend instead on commissioned "sales reps" who handle titles from lots of firms. You might get a double shuffle here.

3. Lastly, you can take heart if neither of the above is the case. If, instead, the company in question uses an

independent distributor, his self-interest in selling your book will match yours and that's good.

4. Remember that while your book may come out of a small house to begin with, it can always have a second coming in a reprint edition by a major house if it is properly promoted and catches on.

5. Remember too, a small firm is likelier to concentrate all its efforts on your book because it does so few books it can't afford *not* to play them *all* like winners.

Likewise, many small firms do a very aggressive high volume mail-order business and, again because they have far fewer titles to be concerned with, are likely to keep your book in print and in circulation much longer than larger houses who have bigger fish to fry.

Big or small, look for a publisher with an active library promotion department since libraries account for more than 50 percent of all trade book sales.

Handling your own career can save you a lot of money.

Negotiating your own contract can get you into a lot of hot water.

Indeed, when your efforts are finally rewarded with a contract, you should run—not walk—to the nearest agent, literary lawyer or at least your friendly family attorney for an opinion and an interpretation.

"Talking money and rights is usually an ordeal... .your [you and your publisher's] aims diverge on the division of profits and risks" says *Publishers Weekly's* Judith Appelbaum.

Contracts come in all shapes, sizes and degrees of air-
ness. They may be as brief as two pages (like Simon and
Schuster's) or as long as twenty. But they almost all routinely contain passages and clauses which are just as
routinely deleted by any astute agent or lawyer.

Only an unrepresented writer would swallow a
"standard" contract whole.

What can you expect to get, speaking in the broadest
terms?

A fine cook does not necessarily shine at reading the
fine print.

Copyrights, for instance.

Copyright: Protecting Your Valuables

Things change in publishing. Not only do agents become editors and publishing houses sink into obliviion
but whole sections of our jurisprudence system shift al-
legiance. It is for this reason that writers are happy they
have agents and to figure out what it all means.

You must always know what your rights are and
where they are. If, for instance, your name and the word
or symbol for copyright appear on the reverse of your
book's title page, your book is properly protected. If the
notice is not there or is in the wrong place, your book
may wind up in "public domain," meaning it's fair
game for any culinary cradle robber.

Even *before* this event your book is protected by "common law copyright." This means it belongs to you and your heirs unless you assign away those rights.

But you'll never understand the game without a scorecard. Do yourself a favor and send for the *Copyright Law Revision* report from the government printing office.

Once covered you are protected for twenty-eight years. Then the copyright can be renewed for *another* twenty-eight years.

Protected from what? Good question, especially since there is the problem of "fair use"—which also can work to your advantage. There is no written description of how extensively one can copy another's work as "fair use" without the owner's permission.

What's out of bounds? If you write a book about pancake cookery and use quite enough material, including recipes, from somebody else's book to harm the sales of that book while increasing (hopefully) the sales of your own, that certainly is not "fair use" and could get you into trouble.

Of course, you would be better off getting written permission from the author before you quote or "borrow" a thing. Short of that, be sure you acknolwedge fully the author and source in your footnotes or bibliography.

Bear in mind, too, that the owner may wish reimbursement for such permission and the law does not set limits on the amounts. Nor will your publisher help you foot the bill if there is one. These matters, however, will not have to be settled until you have a signed contract.

But facts and ideas themselves, like the moon, belong to everyone. It is the *way* they are presented and the style and language employed that you cannot use or have used (if the material is yours) verbatim.

The Contract

1. YOU (the author) are required to deliver a manuscript consisting of
   • a specified number of words
   • typed double-spaced with two clean copies
   • delivered on a specified date to the publisher's office.
2. YOU will agree to an *acceptability clause* requiring that
   • your manuscript in its final form be "acceptable in style, form and content" to the publisher (until this requirement is met you will probably not recive the other half or one-third of your royalty still owed you).
3. YOU will agree (probably) to a *grant of rights*, meaning that you grant the publisher exclusive license to "print, publish and sell" the work in book form in the English language, in the U.S., its territories and possessions, and Canada.

4. THEY (the publishers) will probably ask you to concede a percentage of the world rights, allowing them to sell your book in England and in translations (in which case, without an agent, you are well advised to agree).

5. THEY may request book rights during the *full term of copyright* and all renewals in which case
   • you are advised to comply or fight the "all renewals" clause, but only if assisted by an agent. (Few books stay in print throughout the entire first term copyright which is twenty-eight years.)

6. THEY may request that the work be copywritten in the company's name. YOU should NOT agree.

7. YOU should check to see that the publisher agrees to
   • publish your completed and accepted manuscript during a specified time limit (eighteen months, for example) after which all rights would revert to you.

8. THEY WILL (probably) demand rights to produce and promote the book in any way they see fit. You are well advised to accept this and similarly worded sections.

9. YOU SHOULD REQUEST a clear definition of "out-of-print" and demand that the publisher be obliged to notify you when your book has been officially declared "out-of-print."

10. YOU should try to learn what the retail price of the book and the first print run will be before sig-

ning the contract to simplify contract negotiation of the advance.

11. YOU should always *try to get an advance* with this rule of thumb in mind:

a.) An advance half of which will be paid "on signing," and half on delivery of the completed manuscript. (Although sometimes the money is divided into three payments.)

b.) Royalties payable as soon as profits from sales have covered your book's original costs. You should get a royalty statement which reports the income your book generated over the preceding six-month period. (But don't hold your breath. These statements never arrive sooner than three or four months after that "closing date" and sometimes they are even tardier. Worse, as one literary agency head reported at an Authors' Guild meeting, "Statements are practically always incorrect, some more than others.")

12. YOU should arrange to receive other monies from sale of the book such as

• 10% royalty on first 5,000 copies of hardcover (12 to 15% thereafter)

• 50% of reprint or book club sales

• 75% of the payments for foreign translations.

Chapter VI

Making The Rounds: Finding a Publisher

Agent or no agent, do you really stand a chance with the typical editor at a typical publishing house receiving more than five thousand queries, outlines and manuscripts a year, of which only fifty will be published?

According to cookbook writer and critic Nika Hazelton, "The publishers tell you every cookbook sells well. I don't believe it. Publishers are the most haphazard and antiquated businessmen in the world. They don't know why they do anything. This whole business of cookbooks is just a morass."

It sounds hopeless, but one typical editor says far from it. "Sometimes I ask myself if it would not be sensible to discard my slush pile* and refuse over-the-transom* submissions. However, when I remember all the good manu-

---

*Both designations for unsolicited manuscripts.

scripts I have found among these and all the good authors who have become steadies on my list, I have my answer."

And you have yours.

Now, where should you begin? At the front door (with the "biggies," the major cookbook publishers) or at the side door where they pay small advances, or the back door where maybe all you get is a hearty handshake and lots of moral support?

Well, maybe all three. In fact, you can market yourself simultaneously to all three or take them on one at a time.

Priorities

Your first consideration is not where to send it but where *and* why.

Agreed it would be nice to be published "big" by a big house. You want generous advances, wide distribution and fat profits? Then you want somebody like the Meredith Corporation behind you.

As *The New York Times Book Review* explains:

What accounts for the sales figure gap between 'B.H. & G.' and every other cookbook, is certainly not the quality, but the ways in which it is merchandised. The usual hardcover is sold only in bookstores—or book departments of other stores. In a few cases, it will be picked up by a club, thus doubling or tripling its ultimate sale. Meredith Press, publishers of the Better Homes and

Gardens cookbooks (there are twenty-eight besides the *New Cookbook*), sweeps into additional arenas no regular publisher, with books in a dozen categories, can manage.

Jack Barlass, Meredith's President, admits: 'Our books are marketed like toothpaste...You can find 'B.H.&G.' in drugstores, supermarkets, department stores—where it will be sold in the gourmet and hardware shops, as well as the book department.

In addition, Meredith has a book club and mail-order operation and a premium business, wherein literally millions of copies have been bought by other companies for their own purposes—particularly trading stamp houses, who then exchange a cookbook for supermarket stamps.

In addition, Meredith also uses market research to discover who buys their books and why. As a result, seven of Meredith's cookbooks have sold one million copies each.

But there are thousands of other possibilities as well.

Getting in Touch

1. Prepare your proposal as professionally as possible (see preceding chapter), or if you have a completed manuscript, prepare an equally professional query letter. Have two clean copies made for your files.

2. If you are in a hurry to break into print, prepare both

letter *and* proprosal. (If the people who get the query letter
are interested, they can have the proposal next, assuming
you haven't already sold it to the first receiver.)

3. Now that you've chosen your weapon, pick your target. Read the lists of publishers contained in various
sources (see Appendix 2 and 4) and pick the dozen you
think deserve your best shot (and vice versa). Number
them from one to twelve in terms of desirability.

4. If feasible, make a phone call or drop a note to con-
firm that the company *is* still in the cookbook business. If
the reply is yes, get the editor's name. Type that name into
your cover letter and/or query letter, attach a stamped,
self-addressed envelope (SASE), weigh, and mail to number one on your list. Send your query letter to number two
with a copy of your biography sheet (keep a dozen copies
of the original in your files at all times).

5. Label two file folders. One, *The (your title) Cookbook*, and the other, outline two, letters. Other folders (depending on your project's scope) may be set aside for new
recipes and related materials you intend to include.

In your letter file, make a note of when, where and to
whom your two mailings went. Also, if you are the forget-
ful type, make a note in your diary six weeks hence re-
minding yourself it's time to get in touch again.

6. Six weeks later, drop a note to the publishers you
contacted previously, politely inquiring whether your
manuscript (name) mailed (date) was received and read.
Include a self-addressed postcard to facilitate a quick reply.

7. If your proposal has already been returned (or when as a result of your persistence it comes back), make a note of that, file the letter after carefully analyzing its message, and start all over again with publisher number two.

After The Sale

What about editors?

Writers love them and leave them. But some hang on to theirs because they break all the rules.

"While editors may still give patient counsel on occasion, they simply do not have the time for literary analysis or author tutoring," says literary agent Ann Elmo in *The Writer*, April, 1976.

That's why *Quick and Easy Vegetarian Cookbook* author Bill Manners would "do it again" with *his* editor, Pamela Veley at M. Evans (who made almost no changes in the finished manuscript.) And so would writer Anna Thomas (*The Vegetarian Epicure*), who shares Pamela with them.

What is an editor?

"He is a reader," says editor, publisher and teacher Philip Sloane, "perhaps the author's first real reader. The editor is a specialist about reading. His specialty is what is sufficiently general and common between a possible readership and what the author has to say. The tool he works with is himself. If the author cannot reach him, he can't reach the editor's readership either."

Still, sometimes it is the editor—not the agent—who works the miracles.

Consider the case of pediatrician Lendon Smith. Dr. Smith, author of *Feed Your Kids Right* (a book with 600,000 McGraw Hill hard-covers in print that Dell bought for paperback publication for $600,000), says the real trick behind the success of his book was "having Gladys Carr" as his editor. "A good editor is the key to the whole thing. I'm more of a talker than a writer and I need someone to make what I say read well. A good editor can make anybody look good."

Judith B. Jones, (described by Mimi Sheraton as "the cookbook editor who is responsible for most of the best cookbooks of any given year"), the very epitome of the good editor who makes writers (James Beard, Julia Child and Michael Field among them) look good, says, "A cookbook editor is different in two ways. You get more closely involved in production because you have to make certain the book works with layout, illustrations, ingredients clearly listed... And you are dealing with people who aren't really professional writers..."*

What does an editor do besides correct your manuscript and (except in smaller houses) discourage you from participating too much in the birth and publication of your own book?

It is unlikely, for instance, that you will be consulted

---

*"Judith B. Jones," *Publishers Weekly*, July 9, 1979.

about what artwork or photographs appear in your book or what dust jacket goes around it.

"We didn't see the dust jacket until a few weeks before publication," admit authors Bill and Ruth Ann Manners. Fortunately, they liked it.

"Ideally," says Judith Appelbaum, "an editor will clarify what you have to say, suggest cuts and additions to strengthen the impact of your work, and change nothing unless change means improvement."

Ideally, when your editor is through reading your book and making the best of it, it will be passed on to a copy editor who will correct your spelling and grammar and, generally speaking, put your shaky knowledge of the English language to shame. Any changes you want to make must be included at this point.

After that comes the typesetting and actual production. There is little for you to do at this stage.

After your book ir first set in type, you will receive galley proofs. Any changes you suggest will be costly for everyone at this point.

Remember, deadlines matter.

By the time page proofs are pulled, only the most minor of minor changes are possible.

And how many copies will they publish?

That depends.

If your cookbook comes out as a paperback original, paperbacks now comprise up to 50% of many publishers' lists), first print run may average 30,000 to 50,000 copies.

While the average hardcover cookbook will average 7,000 copies for its first printing.

Knopf's first printing of Julia Child's *Mastering the Art of French Cooking* in 1961 was 10,000 copies.

The first printing of her *Julia Child and Company* however, was 81,000 in hardcover and 300,000 in paper.

Yours might be as small as 2,000, but traditional trade book houses rarely run off fewer than 3,500.

What happens after you actually get yourself between covers, so to speak? God willing, it goes to the stores. Hopefully, that's not the last stop. (Unsold copies, those designated "returns," are shipped back to the publisher. Paperback houses will accept returns at any time while hardcover houses have a time limit of eighteen months.)

A typical "smaller" bookstore in a town of forty thousand people, open every day of the year, might do $200,000 worth of business. (Booksellers buy their stock for 60 percent of cover price) and must pay "freight" as well.

The store will carry anywhere from five thousand to ten thousand titles at any given time. The stock is generally changed three times a year. (A book that sells one hundred copies is considered a big seller.)

Obviously, you and everybody else will have to work fast.

On the other hand, the average cookbook may stay in print for twenty years. It may also eventually be reprinted since 50 percent of the cookbooks from previously unpublished authors are. You could even wind up among that elite 10 percent who get to see their labors of love offered by a book club or go on to foreign editions.

What if, if of all ifs, your book is accepted by the Book of the Month Club? (A magic act for your editor to perform.) Here's what Craig Claiborne and his collaborator got out of it, according to an article in *Publishers Weekly*, August 27, 1979:

> A total of $86,000 has been advanced by the Book-of-the-Month Club for two related volumes originating with *The New York Times* and on the fall list of Times Books. *Craig Claiborne's New York Times Cookbook* has brought $51,000, while *The New York Times 60-Minute Gourmet* by Pierre Franey, who is also collaborator on the Claiborne, accounts for the other $35,000. There are additional sales of the latter to the Cooking and Crafts and Better Homes and Gardens Book Clubs and *Woman's Day*.

What if, as few of us do, you never reach that pinnacle? What if you never even break through at Harper & Row or sell more than one hundred copies? Is there life after a Simon & Schuster turndown? Indeed.

Get-Yourself-Published Possibilities

One way to get yourself published is to explore common grounds. A large corporation, for instance, might be interested enough to publish you. If not your book—maybe *theirs.*

Jeanne Jones was a natural for The Batter-Lite Foods Company, manufacturers of low-cal, low-sodium food items, since she had already done a low-sodium cookbook on her own. So Batter-Lite created three Jeanne Jones Cookbooks for their "library," helping *her* reputation and theirs.

"It is my estimate," says company president Bruce L. Samlan, "that we sold approximately fifty thousand of these books over the last four and one half years. Most were sold to tie in along with our products or were offered on the box or through the enclosed insertion."

How about getting yourself an angel? Somebody who will foot the bills because he/she/it stands to benefit from the book as well as you. Are you a vegetarian or Seventh Day Adventist? Maybe the National Vegetarian Association or the Seventh Day Adventists would like to publish your book. Is your book about herbs? Why not approach an herb-lovers group or the Horticultural Society of America?

Even your local church might be persuaded to become your benefactor if your book can be turned into a fund-raising collection of church members' recipes which you edit and oversee.

Another "angel" possibility is a large kitchenwares supplier. Here's how Washington, D.C.'s Kitchen Bazaar, a store that does big business with happy cookers off the street and through the mails described one of *their* in-house projects, a book by their own on-the-premises culinary expert:

IT'S FINALLY HERE! KITCHEN BAZAAR'S
NOSTALGIC COLLECTION OF
WORLDWIDE FAMILY FAVORITES—
"RECIPES TO RONA"!

When Rona sent out the call to our customers for favorite recipes handed down from generation to generation in their families...she underestimated the response by a "landslide." Even after testing all of the entries and tossing out those that didn't measure up, Rona still got enough "grist" for two books. So this is volume one of what will be a two-volume series. It's a great book for gift-giving (to others or to yourself!)...over three hundred pages packed full of delicious "hand-me-down" recipes submitted by our many friends across the country and around the world...

> Softback, $6.95
> Available Dec. 1

Would a gourmet shop in *your* area like to back a Rona of their own?

If you are writing a book with a special focus anyway, there's no reason why your court of *last* resort shouldn't be your first. Suppose you are doing a collection of recipes from the time of Da Vinci. Rather than Beacon Press, you ought to send your proposal to the Boston Museum of Fine Arts first. Maybe you'd meet with more success if your manuscript went to the Metropolitan Museum of Art in New York. The Met has successfully published three historical recipe collections by Lorna J. Sass.

Another way to break into print is to hitch your wagon to a star. This method produces books which author Nika Hazelton scathingly refers to as "books where the 'Writer' just goes to the food publicity people (the coffee council, peanut council) and throws together their mimeographed recipes into something between two covers." And then, says Hazelton, "The most infuriating thing of all, you meet your own already published recipes, even the ones with mistakes, coming and going in these people's cookbooks."

One of the "Writers" she deprecates, the most successful of his breed, is William I. Kaufman who believes that books can be a commodity. Kaufman has written more than forty books about cooking with everything from peanut butter to garlic to cottage cheese and chocolate.

Kaufman finds a publisher with no difficulty usually Doubleday), then proceeds to assemble a book from various food councils' publicity releases, his own vast files of recipes, and any other available sources.

The more "zeroed-in," i.e., single-food-specific, your book is, the easier it may be to get yourself into print since it stands to reason that the Banana Council is bound to be interested in anybody who has dreamed up one hundred new ways to use bananas.

In Kaufman's case, his blender cookbook prompted a blender company to buy lots of books for their customers. Likewise, a million copies of his *Sugar-free Cookbook* were purchased by an artificial sweetner company for sale by mail.

There's no reason why a book with sponsorship should be any less "honorable" than a book done in any other fashion. It's not just what you do, after all, but the way that you do it, too.

Even libraries wear two caps these days. "Yes, we publish, too," says the headline in an ad placed by the Boston Public Library in the trade publication *Library Journal.* Newspapers, too, often have book publishing units. *The New York Times,* for instance, runs Times Books (formerly Quadrangle) which puts out a varied list that in the past has included a number of basic how-to cooking books on wine, cheese and more. Likewise, *The San Francisco Chronicle* also sponsors Chronicle Books, a company that buys cookbooks on occasion.

Rejection and After

What if you've put in your thumb, not once but a dozen or more times, but you still haven't pulled out any plums?

Remember, if you are feeling rejected, you are not alone. You are, in fact, cooking on the front burner with the rest of the majority.

According to a report by The Unpublished Library, a publishing company catering to publish-it-yourselfers, 93 percent of all books (that means 93 percent of all cookbooks as well) produced in any given year are rejected by publishers.

As one Midwest author of a mail-order cookbook put it, "Of the fifty publishers I submitted my query to, three were interested. But I received only one real contract out of the three responding." Not an atypical experience.

Should you throw in the kitchen towel? Should you give up the idea that one of those three to five new titles the typical cookbook collector buys next year will be yours?

What is it that editors, publishers and agents want that you haven't got? At least so far?

Rejection slips may or may not be interpreted as danger signals. Take a close look at yours.

"If the author gets even two or three consistent criticisms," says Elaine Gill, the co-owner of the Crossing Press, "he certainly should give thought to revision of the material...but as to retiring the manuscript...the number of submissions to be made depends entirely on the stamina of the author."

Here are some of the constant comments editors make, what they mean and what to do about them.

A. Dear Mrs. Goulart:
Thank you for your submission. Unfortunately we will have to disappoint you. Given the competitive nature of the cookbook market we cannot add another title on the same subject to our list. There is the further complication that your style is a little too off-beat for Doubleday purposes. We tend to publish more conservative cookbooks without the literary frills you employ...

One down. There is no hope here since the publisher offers three major objections to the idea. Make a note to try them again a year from now if you still have the book. By then, either the editor will have changed or your book will have.

B. Dear Frances,
Thanks very much for sending in your proposal for a vegetarian weight loss cookbook. Unfortunately I have to tell you that Viking already has a somewhat similar book in the works, and our cookbook list is small enough that we don't feel we can undertake two vegetarian books at once—so I must regretfully say no to your project. But it's such a good idea (if somewhat special) that I'm sure you'll have no difficulty placing it elsewhere...

This bodes well. When an editor tells you you have "a good idea," take note. Flattery may get you somewhere—at least, if not with this house, with another. Write to the editor, say thanks, and politely inquire whether she has any house in mind you ought to try (enclose a stamped, self-addressed envelope.)

C. Dear Ms. Goulart:
   We have completed our review of your idea. Although it's a very good idea and contains many intriguing suggestions, we feel that the sales interest is somewhat removed from mainstream America. For our purposes, we need to publish cookbooks that have a broader appeal. I return your two manuscripts. Thank you for sending them to us...

Definitely worth a follow-up note or phone call to inquire whether the editor would look again if you rewrote the book for "broader appeal."

How can you give rejection slips the slip?
1. Big or small, editors seem to think they rarely get what is coming to them, namely an original idea.
"You should spend ar much time searching for the unique concept as in writing it," insist the husband-and-wife team who run Meadowbrook Press in Wayzata, Minnesota.

One good example?

How about Barbara M. Walker of Ossining, New York. "When she and her four-year-old daughter read the Laura Ingalls Wilder children's books," says a Gannett newspaper report, "she decided to find out how some of the pioneer dishes mentioned could be prepared in a contemporary kitchen."*

Barbara's book (her first), *The Little House Cookbook*, came out of a major house (Harper and Row). But Julie Jordan's (*Wings of Life*) didn't. "We look for a cookbook idea that is novel," says her publisher, John Gill of the Crossing Press. "If not novel at least extraordinarily competent."

According to Judith Jones (herself an extraordinary cook, say friends), "I don't think a cookbook deserves to be published unless it makes a genuine contribution and is the work of a dedicated cook who really has something new to say . . . too many cookbooks are published without a raison d'etre . . . I'm looking for original voices, writers with a strong original flair, who have something to say about food."

2. Can a good idea be good the second time around? It's tough but not impossible. For example, how about another basic book, another "kitchen bible." As James Beard

---

Fair Press, November 28, 1979.

has observed, there are only so many basic recipes in the world; the rest are variations. "A cookbook has to be really original and terribly well written to intrigue me. Almost none are," he says (*New York Times Magazine*, December 24, 1978).

On the other hand, it's certainly worth a try.

"It is the dream of every publisher to come up with a big basic cookbook that will rival *The Joy of Cooking*," says reviewer Mimi Sheraton. "This [*The Fannie Farmer Cookbook*, revised edition] is Knopf's move in that direction."

Proof that there's always room for one more of the same, another bread book, for instance, was Mel London's *Bread Winners* described by *New York Daily News* reporter Suzanne Hamlin as "an extraordinary new cookbook—a collection of photographs and recipes from real cooks across the country, people who bake bread because they love it."

3. How can you tell if you are on target with your title?

It's possible you need to do a title search. Maybe your book's fine and the title isn't. What can you do?

Barring a tin ear, you should be able to come up with a new and better one or an alternative in case.

For inspiration, check out the winners in the R. T. French Tastemaker Awards competition, the only national awards competition honoring cookbook authors. Here, for instance, are a few of the winners in 1977.

Best Cook Book:

General/Basic	*James Beard's Theory and Practice of Good Cooking* (Knopf)
American/Regional	*The Flavor of the South* Jeanne A. Voltz (Doubleday)
European Cooking	*Great Cooks and Their Recipes: From Taillevant to Escoffier* Anne Willan (McGraw-Hill)
International Cuisine/Best Cookbook-First Time Author	*The Key to Chinese Cooking* Irene Kuo (Knopf)
Specialty	*Book of Great Cookies* Maida Heatter (Knopf)
Natural Foods/Special Diets	*A Celebration of Vegetables* Robert Ackart (Atheneum)
Original Soft Cover	*The Book of Salads* Sonia Uvezian (101 Productions)

4. *The Recipes*

   One element that *is* optional, but is something to consider, especially if you've got those rejection-slips-what-next blues, is suggested by Dean and Nancy Tudor in their book, *Cooking for Entertaining:*

Extra information is often desirable, such as complementary wines, suitable prefaces (soups, salads, vegetables, etc.), make-ahead preparation, seasonal variations, ease of freezing, perhaps calories and approximate costs of the meal, and, of course, how many persons can be fed, and some indication of level of expertise. Additionally, the cost of the recipes can be worked out by dividing the price of the book by the number of recipes. For an excellent discussion on recipe appraisal, read Margaret Batjer's *Meals for the Modern Family* (Wiley, 1961), pp. 110-126.

5. *Do You Have a Badly Typed Proposal (Manuscript)?*

Not paying attention to details can wind up costing you plenty.

"Clean typing, double-spacing and adequate margins" is the advice from Benton Arnovitz at Stein & Day which all queried editors echoed.

"Use a new black ribbon and a standard format," urges agent Lea Braff.

6. *Lack of Readability or Workability*

Your proposal must have readability. Cross-references in the text should be avoided. When cooking the reader really can't flip back and forth. If menus are given, then page references to the recipe should be given in the same space.

And even though they *do* get published, "an unbroken stream of junky ingredients and misguided short cuts does invalidate a cookbook," says book and magazine food writer Anne Mendelson.

7. It may be that your writing isn't as good as your good idea.

One way to remedy that is to take a writing course or attend a writers' conference. (They are held annually in every state and writers' reference books tell you how to get in touch.)

"I believe that for me," says William Sloane in *The Craft of Writing* (Norton and Company, 1979), "the greatest single experience was dealing, each year, with ten or a dozen unsuccessful writers, people with troubles that they had not been able to solve...I began to notice that these writers were, by my standards, far from hopeless...I think a thumping 10 percent of all of them went away, revised, worked on their books with their eyes open, and got published in fairly short order. Any editor will tell you that nowhere near 10 percent of his manuscripts are salvageable within the editorial office and process."*

Rewriting, Rethinking

If you've decided to rewrite, consider the possibility of:
1. An entirely new market. Maybe your book could be retargeted for the juvenile or young adult market.

Another possibility is:

2. To send your as-is or rewritten proposal abroad. Have you thought about a Canadian, Hawaiian, Australian, or British publisher? It may not be the long shot you think.

3. Or maybe you can add the imprimatur of some VIP? It couldn't hurt to try.

Mrs. Eugene N. Chardral of Flint, Michigan, likes to tell about the cookbook she and a church group were preparing that "cried out" for a particular already-published James Beard recipe. Mrs. C. wrote to Mr. B. for permission. The prestigious author wrote "okay" on her letter and mailed it back.

It may not happen to you. But such acts of creative agression are certainly worth a gamble.

4. Revise it, but get a second, even a third opinion.

Bookstore proprietors and librarians whose business is also books and their buyers are two good possibilities for a second or third opinion.

Two more?

Get friendly with editors on the women's pages at your local newspapers, or local catering firms or restaurants.

Don't give every opinion equal weight, but the repetition of a criticism gives you a good clue as to what may be wrong especially if it is an echo of an editorial criticism you've already heard.

5. Print it yourself.

Do a low-cost mimeographed or Xeroxed limited edition version of your book, advertise it and sell it by mail.

It's cheaper than you think and if the "biggies" *never* bite, you'll still have a book to your credit.

6. On the other hand, if you need lots of literary TLC, there are over five hundred freelance editors and editorial consultants listed in *Literary Market Place* alone, cross-indexed by specialities (such as manuscript analysis, rewriting, etc.) who can help you cut your own mustard.

Chapter VII

Pulling Your Own Apron Strings: Promoting The Book, Promoting Yourself

There is no better way to learn the ropes of your profession then to pull your own strings. It takes a little time but it pays off.

"If I write an article in *The Times* on a woman who cooks shrimp," says Craig Claiborne, "next day she'll be called by every publisher in New York to write *the* definitive shrimp cookbook."

Of course, unless you've got *something* going for you, it's unlikely Craig Claiborne (or anybody else) will write about you.

If you don't know enough about cooking, take lessons. If you know too much, teach.

You never know where such experiences can lead you.

Here's Marion Cunningham's story. She's the woman

responsible for the latest *Fannie Farmer Cookbook*, 1979's big recipe collection.

["I took lessons] from everybody who offered them—European or Chinese—on the West Coast," including Cecilia Chiang, owner of the Mandarin Restaurant in San Francisco. Ms. Cunningham now teaches cooking in her *own* home and has taught in Aspen, Colo., Pasadena, Calif., and in James Beard's classes in New York. She has also taught with Mr. Beard at the Gritti Palace in Venice. As a result, she says, she enjoyed "two of the most exhilarating times in [my] life, the occasions [I] cooked for Michel Guerard and Jean Troisgros, two of Europe's most celebrated chefs,...when they were giving lessons at Michael James's cooking school in the Napa Valley."

She continues, "It had to be something American. For Jean Troisgros I made California-style vegetable soup, a simple roast chicken and bread and butter pudding...For Guerard I made a Walnut Creek cioppino, the fish soup that is so widely known in California—with scallops, cod, prawns and clams. Plus corn sticks and pecan pie. I've never been so flattered. He asked me for the pecan pie recipe."*

What have *you* got to offer? Can you rise to the top like the bread you're so famous for? Are your chances of breaking into print or into the big time with what you've

---

*New York Times, September 12, 1978, p. 64

got in print very good if you don't have a degree? What if you don't have anything but a flair for food?

Parlay it! If you've got it, flaunt it. And if you haven't got it? Fake it. Anyone who can stretch a hamburger for two into a meatloaf for six ought to be able to work some simple look-good magic.

Robert Carrier, for instance, whose best seller *Great Dishes of the World* has sold over two million copies and appeared in eleven languages, rose to the top of a profession he never trained for. Today he is not only one of Britain's foremost food experts but a columnist, TV celebrity and, of late, a restauranteur.

Nor did the now-successful Dolores Casella have much going for her to begin with. When she started she didn't even have a high school education. Her first sale was a recipe contest in a local newspaper. She collected a pile of rejection slips before she sold an article to a national magazine. But eventually she sold two cookbooks, *A World of Breads* and *A World of Baking*, and has published ever since, supporting herself and her children with royalties and article sales.

Similarly, San Francisco writer Jacqueline Killeen made the switch from publicity director at an art museum to cookbook writer when she quit to write a restaurant guide, *101 Nights in California*. Not only did she write it, but, since nobody would buy it, she published it herself with the help of her partner-husband, Ray, who designed and illustrated the book as well. Today the Killeens have a small but aggressive and prosperous company devoted largely to publishing cookbooks.

And Vicki Lansky, a young mother, and five other mothers wrote a book, *Feed Me, I'm Yours*, as a fund-raiser for the Childbirth Education Association of Minneapolis-St. Paul. The CEA wasn't prepared to handle the flood of orders for the book on feeding small children, so Mrs. Lansky and her husband made a business of it, starting the Meadowbrook Press, which now publishes Mrs. Lansky's and other authors' cookbooks. Her second book, *Taming the C.O.O.K.Y. Monster*, hit *The New York Times* best-seller list three weeks after publication.

If the Meadowbrook Press adds you to their list, "We do everything in our power to see to it that it meets or beats our average sales per book of two hundred thousand copies," says Bruce Lansky, the firm's president and editor-in-chief. That's a lot, say most other sources. Generally speaking, two thousand might be considered not so hot while ten thousand copies is a good, if not great, sale.

But if your publisher doesn't hustle, then most of the look-at-me locomotion will be up to you.

As Judith Appelbaum and Nancy Evans, the authors of *How to Get Happily Published* (Harper & Row), put it:

Your primary goal between the day your manuscript is accepted and the day it's published should be to get everyone—from your editor to the publicity director to the sales department personnel—involved with (and, if you can manage it, excited about) the future of your book. To make them envision that future the way you want it to happen, you'll have to reinforce and supplement the marketing suggestions you made in your original proposal through occasional short, informal notes to your editor.

Shaking the Money Tree

If you're whipping up everything in your three-star kitchen except fame and a good living, don't despair. You don't have to perish before you publish.

For instance, there are a number of ways to generate income and promote your published or unpublished project simultaneously.

1. It helps to have a *gimmick*. Why? Newspapers, magazines, the media, in other words, take notice of you. Without them, you may have a book, but not a best-seller or even a fair seller.

Sally and Jane Nichols, a mother-and-daughter team, have so far turned their culinary gimmick into a restaurant chain, but it could just as well have been a book (and may well be yet). Said *Woman's Day* (February 20, 1979), reporting on their success:

"Have you eaten a flowerpot today?" The question may sound a little daffy, but seven days a week there are enough people in the vicinity of Atlanta, Georgia, who can answer it with a satisfied yes to assure Jane and Sally Nichols of a substantial annual profit. In just four years their "flowerpot sandwiches" have enabled the enterprising mother-daughter team to open three busy eateries that are currently grossing $1.5 million a year. "My daughter Sally is the innovator," Jane Nichols proudly acknowledges. "The recipes, ideas for decor, all the creative aspects are hers. I just supervise operations and make sure things run smooth."

2. Teach cooking. Helen Worth, originator of the Learn Your Lunch series in Manhattan and author of the book *Cooking Without Recipes* admits, "I majored in playwriting." But it hasn't stopped her from charging (and getting) $75 an hour for a private cooking lesson and advances that are no doubt equally amazing for her books.

Credentials

It doesn't hurt to have credentials as an instructor. And lots of cooks teach to finance their writing. Or teach until they sell. Cookbook people with impeccable credentials like Diana Kennedy (*The Tortilla Book*), and Perla Meyers (*The Seasonal Kitchen*), and even the redoubtable James Beard teach. Besides cash, this experience gives you credibility in the eyes of editors.

Where to teach? Everywhere from your State Agricultural Home Extension Service to the local Y, Continuing Education, Senior Citizen Centers, catering services, cookware shops, even unlikelier institutions like the electric and gas companies sponsor cooking classes and workshops in various seasons for various reasons.

If your book is about garden greenery, you could do what one writer did. Expert Maida Silverman talks about holly, mistletoe, ivy, cloves, nutmeg, other spices and plants of the season. Horticultural Society of New York, 128 West 58th St. 12/5. 6:30-8. Advance registration necessary on this. At the Queens Botanical Garden. (Notice from a magazine "Events" column.)

3. Run your own ads. The price of an ad is often quite modest and definitely pay for itself. In *Bestways*, a health magazine sold nationally, twenty-five words is $32.50 with a per line charge of $1.30 thereafter. That's where Circus Publications of Phoenix, Arizona, sold their three-dollar *Gourmet Treats Cookbook*. It's a thousand to one shot your publisher will ever buy space anywhere on your behalf. So be your own best friend, you never know what might happen.

4. Write magazine and newspaper articles based on your research and the material already presented in your proposal.

Make a list of possible markets, write a brief description of the article and send it off. You can do this to generate a little income *before* you sell the book or after.

Published articles on the topic you're trying to sell as a book are good selling tools in themselves. Any articles that get into print can be added to your proposal.

5. Explore tie-ins no matter how farfetched to further your sales and/or to promote yourself and your book.

Here, for example, from a New York newspaper is the kind of bright marketing idea any editor is guaranteed to at least consider, if not to execute on behalf of your book.

Dean & DeLuca has put together an exotic dried mush-room sampler: Italian porcini, French cepes, Swiss chanterelles, French morels and Polish mushroom caps are each packed in a one-ounce tin. *The Mushroom Feast*, a supberb cookbook by Jane Grigson, is in-cluded, all for $35.

Minuha Cannon, author of *The Fructose Cookbook* (East Woods Press), found a natural outlet for her paper-back title through Batter-Lite Foods, a manufacturer of diet products including fructose. The company has sold a half million of the cookbooks.

Your for-sale-by-mail book might even get a big push from a large circulation magazine that likes it as much as you do.

Tom Morton's *All Kids' Natural Food Cookbook*, which the All Kids' Day Care Center in East Lansing, Michigan, published, got a three-page plug in *Family Circle* (March 3, 1979). This made the $3.95 book a quick sellout.

6. Visit bookstores and any outlet where they do—or will—handle your book.

Another successful hornblower is Carla Emery, author of *Carla Emery's Old-Fashioned Recipe Book*. Thanks almost entirely to the author's efforts, the book is now available in a large-format paperback from Bantam Books. Mrs. Emery was interviewed by *New York Times* reporter Richard Lingeman in the midst of a ninety-two-city, four-month tour by camper, accompanied by six children and a goat.

> It began in 1970, when Mrs. Emery, deciding to earn some money, drew up a table of contents of a book that would include recipes and tell how to do old-fashioned things like canning, quilt-making, and tanning (to name a few). She then took ads in several magazines. A lot of people sent in their money, and Mrs. Emery found herself with a bad case of guilt on her hands. She wrote the book (it took four years before she was an "honest woman" again), mimeographed it on colored paper—"the kind churches use for their Sunday bulletins"—and assembled it with the help of her neighbors. Stimulated by Mrs. Emery's family promotion tours in the van to country and state fairs, sales reached fifty-thousand copies, the book went through several editions and be-

came "the second largest industry in Kendrick" (the first is seed). Then Mrs. Emery sold the paperback rights to Bantam for $115,000 (she retains the right to sell her edition by mail).

Lingeman doesn't mention it but the book sold extremely well, even by mail, *in spite* of the high $12.95 price tag.

And how about Lady Harlech? No doubt it doesn't hurt to be a member of the upper crust if you want to seel 'em (she moved eight thousand copies of her book *Feast Without Fusss* in eleven weeks), but the author's editor says that's not what did it. "It was Pamela herself who sold the book," says editor Judith Kern at Atheneum. "She is a glamorous woman with an attractive personality and also an excellent cook." You too should be able to hit two out of the three if you try.

Some good reasons these good works should be done— and done good and fast.

Because:

1. "In the conflict-ridden area of publicity, advertising and sales, as Judith Appelbaum observes, "you will have to convince them that you don't fit the conventional writer's mold."

2. "Publishers," says Lee Dembart in *The New York Times*, "accept returns on hardcover books up to eighteen months after they have been shipped. If a book has been around longer than eighteen months the bookseller either

puts it on special or takes it home." (Unless, of course, a book club picks it up or a paperback house makes a whopping bid.)

3. How about a promotion tour? Maybe your publisher will foot the bill and maybe he won't.* If not, why not hot foot it around your own hometown on your own?

How to Arrange Your Own Autographing Party

1. Find a likely locale and work out the details. A bookstore is the most logical choice. So is a library. But a health food store (if that's what your book deals with), a nature center, a cookware shop, a cheese and herb outlet, etc. are all alternate possibilities. (If it is part of a chain and it is successful, you can repeat it at other stores in the chain).

2. Make arrangements with your publisher to deliver copies of your book well in advance of the date you pick.

3. Make signs for the store window and a few to post elsewhere in town.

4. Run a small ad, like the following, in your local paper—publicizing yourself, your book, and the store. The publicity (and the business it produces) alone should be payment enough for your host.

---

*"To do a really good promotional job for an author would cost $20,000," says Dave X. Manners who promoted his brother's book for much less on a much smaller scale.

YOU ARE CORDIALLY INVITED
to
MEET THE AUTHOR OF
(*YOUR BOOK*)
AT
THE NATURAL LIVING CENTER
33 Danbury Road, Wilton, Ct.
1:00 - 2:00 SATURDAY, JUNE 14th
(Your name) will autograph copies of her new book
(hard and softcover versions both on sale) and demon-
strate sugarfree candy and snack making
FREE...NO RESERVATIONS NECESSARY

5. Write a release like the following, have copies made
and mail or hand deliver them to local radio, TV, and
newspaper people—even those who might be only margin-
ally concerned—well in advance of your party date. Write
a personal invitation in red on the top of each invitation
sent to a press person.

Your name
address
phone #

FOR IMMEDIATE RELEASE PLEASE

(YOUR NAME) AUTOGRAPHS HER BOOK
"NUTRITION IN A NUTSHELL"

AT NORWALK COMMUNITY COLLEGE, (DATE)
PUBLIC INVITED
(Your name) author of (*your book*) will autograph
copies of her book at a party at Norwalk Community
College Evening School, (address), on (date). The public is invited.
(Your name), who lives at (your address), has written a
guide to the healthful foods still remaining on supermarket shelves. Included are such topics as: the choles-
terol controversy: sugar, salt and fats; and dieting with
nature's wonder foods.
Festivities will be held from 1:00-2:30 in Room ____ of
the college. There is no fee. Refreshments—including
take-home samples of recipes in (your name) book will
be provided for all. No purchase necessary.
For further information call ____.

6. A few days before the party make a personal phone
call to the people you most want to have in attendance—
i.e., the women's page editors and book reviewers.

7. Provide refreshments and take-home samples of a
few of your specialities from the book.

Your publisher will pay for press releases and may even
foot the entire bill if he's feeling flush. Or, see if the shop-
keeper will provide refreshments free.

APPENDIX 1

Selling Like Hot Cakes:
The Best Selling Cookbooks from 1895 to 1975

Title	*Copies Sold*
Better Homes and Gardens Cook Book. 1930, Meredith	18,684,976
Betty Crocker's Cookbook. 1950, Golden Press	13,000,000
The Joy of Cooking, Irma S. Rombauer and Marion Rombauer Becker. 1931, Bobbs-Merrill, Inc.	8,992,700
The Good Housekeeping Cookbook, ed. by Zoe Coulson. Good Housekeeping Books	5,250,000
The Pocket Cook Book, by Elizabeth Woody. 1942, Pocket Books	4,900,000
The Boston Cooking School Cook Book, by Fannie Farmer. 1896, Little, Brown	
Better Homes and Gardens Meat Cook Book, 1959, Meredith	3,609,105
The American Woman's Cook Book, ed. by Ruth Berolzheimer. 1939, Doubleday	3,549,276
The I Hate to Cook Book, by Peg Bracken. 1960, Harcourt Brace Jovanovich	2,929,782
Better Homes and Gardens Casserole Cook Book. 1961, Meredith	2,613,948
The Weight Watchers Program Cookbook, by Jean Nidetch. 1973, Hearthside	2,575,000

Title	*Copies Sold*
Better Homes and Gardens Barbecue Book. 1956, Meredith	2,439,001
Betty Crocker's Good and Easy Cookbook. 1954, Simon and Schuster	2,400,000
Better Homes and Gardens Salad Book. 1958, Meredith	2,341,060
Let's Cook It Right, by Adelle Davis. 1947, Harcourt Brace Jovanovich	2,151,439
Better Homes and Gardens Fondue and Tabletop Cooking. 1970, Meredith	2,022,529

APPENDIX 2

To Market, To Market

Ninety percent of the country's publishing houses (representing 80 percent of the industry as a whole) put out one to several dozen cookbooks a year. Furthermore, there are three times as many cookbooks published today as there were a decade ago. It's a boom market, and here's how to make it work for you.

You can try the A list or the B list or both, depending on how much an advance and/or a "prestige" publisher matters to you. (Addresses are in any of the books on publishing listed in Appendix 4.)

List A—Prestige publishers and/or houses who pay advances of at least $500 plus royalties

A & W Inc.
Atheneum
Avon Books
Bantam Books
Charter Books
Thomas Y. Crowell Co., Inc.
Delacorte Press
Dell Publishing Co., Inc.
Dodd, Mead & Co.

Doubleday & Co., Inc.
E. P. Dutton
M. Evans & Co., Inc.
Farrar, Strauss & Giroux
Follett Publishing Co.
H. P. Books
Harcourt Brace Jovanovich, Inc.
Harper & Row, Publishers, Inc.
Holt, Rinehart & Winston
Houghton Mifflin Co.
Jove Books
Alfred A. Knopf, Inc.
Lane Publishing Co.
J. B. Lippincott Co.
Little, Brown & Co.
MacMillan Pub. Co., Inc.
McGraw-Hill Book Co.
David McKay Co., Inc.
Meredith Corp.
William Morrow & Co., Inc.
New American Library
Pantheon Books, Inc.
Pocket Books
Prentice-Hall, Inc.
G. P. Putnam's Sons
Random House, Inc.
Rodale Press
St. Martin's Press, Inc.

Charles Scribner's Sons
Simon & Schuster
Stein and Day
The Viking Press
Warner Books

List B—Publishers with limited funds and limited resources. No advance or small advances plus royalty

Baronet Publishing Co.
Barron's Educational Series, Inc.
Butterick Publications
Celestial Arts
Contemporary Books
Crossing Press
The Devin-Adair Co.
Garden Way Pub. Co.
Stephen Greene Press
Keats Publishing Company, Inc.
Meadowbrook Press
101 Publications
Oxmoor House, Inc.
Parker Publishing Co., Inc.
Price/Stern/Sloan Publishers, Inc.
Quick Fox, Inc.
Henry Regnery Co.
Rutledge Books

Charles E. Tuttle Co., Inc.
Two Continents Publishing Group, Ltd.
Walker & Co.
Woodbridge Press Publishing Co.
Workman Publishing Co., Inc.

List C—Publishers who fall somewhere in between or whose policies may be unpredictable

Arco Publishing Co., Inc.
Chilton Book Co.
Crown Publishers, Inc.
Dover Publications, Inc.
Penguin
Rawson Wade Associates Publishers, Inc.
Stackpole Books
Times Books

APPENDIX 3

Boning Up: Books for Cooks

There's a lot you don't know. But you don't know how *much* you don't know until you get started on your book. Fortunately there are a lot of places to turn for help in looking it up, tracking it down, talking it out face to face, or by mail or phone.

Examine the gaps in your gastronomic background. What books constitute a basic library for the would-be cookbook author? Then look at the gaps in your writing background—what do you need to know to be a typewriter cook?

Cookbooks For Reference and Pleasure

"What dozen basic cookbooks would I choose if I were on a desert island?" asks Julia Child. "I can't do it! I can't thin down to a dozen. I'm a bibliomane, I must admit, when it comes to cookbooks. I need them for my profession, I profess. I have to create my own research center—that's my excuse. I would simply die without my library, and would just have to take it with me, desert island or no."

Some of her favorites as listed in the October 1977 issue of *Book Views,* include:

The Joy of Cooking, Irma Rombauer and Marion Becker, Bobbs-Merrill Co., Inc., $10. New American Library one-volume paperback, $4.95, or two volumes at $1.95 each.

American Heritage Cookbook, the editors of *American Heritage,* Bantam paperback, $1.95.

Gourmet Cookbooks (Published by *Gourmet* magazine, at $18 each or $35 for two volumes).

New York Times Cookbooks, edited by Craig Claiborne, Times Books, $10 and $12.50.

Time-Life American Cooking series (eight regional books and a general American Cooking book at $9.95 each).

James Beard's Theory and Practice of Good Cooking, James Beard Knopf, $12.95.

Escoffier Cookbook, Crown, $6.95, and *Larousse Gastronomique The French Menu Cookbook,* Richard Olney, Simon and Schuster, $10.

Simple French Food, Richard Olney, Atheneum, $12.50.

Mastering The Art of French Cooking, Volumes I and II Knopf.

The French Chef Cookbook, Julia Child, Knopf, $8.95 and Bantam paperback, $1.95.

Uniform Retail Meat Identity Standards and Barbara Bloch's *The Meat Board Meat Book,* McGraw-Hill.

Cutting Up in The Kitchen, Merele Ellis, Chronicle Books paperback, $5.95.

Other books not on Julia's list, but which might be on yours are:

Beard, James. *Beard on Food*. New York: Knopf, 1974.

——— *Delights and Pleasures*. New York: Atheneum, 1964.

Forsman, John, ed. *Recipe Index: The Eater's Guide to Periodical Literature, 1970*. Detroit: Gale, 1973.

Hazelton, Nika. *I Cook As I Please*. New York: Grosset & Dunlap, 1975.

Jones, Evan *American Food: The Gastronomic Story*. New York: Dutton, 1975.

Kleeman, Elayne J. and Voltz, Jeanne. *How to Turn a Passion for Food into a Profit*. New York: Rawson Wade, 1979.

Norman, Barbara. *Tales of the Table: A History of Western Cuisine*. Englewood Cliffs, N.J.: Prentice-Hall, 1972.

Page, Edward B. and Kingsford, P. W. *The Master Chefs: A History of Haute Cuisine*. New York: St. Martin's Press, 1971.

Patten, Marguerite. *Books for Cooks: A Bibliography of Cookery*. New York: R. R. Bowker, 1975.

Shannon, Ellen. *The Cook in the Kitchen: A Dictionary of Culinary Terms*. South Brunswick, N.J.: A. S. Barnes, 1973.

Tannahill, Reay. *Food in History*. New York: Stein and Day, 1973.

Tudor, Nancy and Dean. *Cooking for Entertaining*. New York: R. R. Bowker, 1976.

Cooking Magazines

There are many periodicals devoted to food. A big city library should have most if not all of the following:

Bon Appetit
Cookbook Digest
Cooking
Cuisine
Food & Wine
Gourmet
Petits Propos Culinaires
The Pleasure of Cooking
Wok Talk

When you find one that does a good job of covering *your* specialty, subscribe.

Book Clubs

By all means join a book club, especially if it has a cooking and crafts section.

Appendix 4

Reference: Publishing in General

Perhaps the best investment you can make to keep yourself up on what's cooking with the competition (can you afford *not* to know that someone else has just sold a cookbook with the same name and subject matter as yours?) is a subscription to:

Publisher's Weekly (PW)
R. R. Bowker Company
1180 Avenue of the Americas
New York, N.Y. 10036

(Also available to read on the premises at any library).

Bowker, (address above) also publishes the following:

• *Book Publishing - What It Is - What It Does* ($11.95). Most libraries stock it—but it's worth purchasing if you are serious.

• *Publishers and Distributors of the United States* ($7.50).

• *Literary Market Place (LMP)*, issued every other year by the Bowker Company. All libraries carry it.

LMP is the "phone book" of the trade publishing industry.

Other sources of information include:

• *Paperback Parnassus* - Roger H. Smith, Westview Press, $12.95.

• *Writer's Market* is issued annually. Most libraries stock it. The address is:
Writer's Digest
9933 Alliance Road
Cincinnati, Ohio 45242
• The Authors Guild
234 West 44th Street
New York, N. Y. 10036

• The Society of Authors' Representatives Inc. (SAR) will send you a pamphlet, *The Literary Agent*, free upon request with a self-addressed, stamped envelope. This is a short but reliable list of literary agents who are members of SAR. To qualify for membership, an agency may not charge fees and must show proof of sales to established trade publishing houses. (Remember, while all members of SAR are reputable, many excellent literary agents are not members.)

SAR has also drawn up two "ideal" contracts, one for U.S. book publication, one for foreign publication, to acquaint you with rights that can be withheld from a publisher. Copies of these contracts are available for 50 cents each plus postage.

SAR's address is 101 Park Avenue, New York, N. Y. 10017.

Also worth reading, even buying is:
• *How to Get Happily Published* by Judith Appelbaum and Nancy Evans (Harper & Row).

Appendix 5

A Potpourri of Sources

Reprints

• Shops specializing in cookbooks both out-of-print and current are:
The Corner Book Shop
102 Fourth Avenue
New York, N. Y.

Quinion Books
541 Hudson Street
New York, N. Y.

• Dover Books, 181 Varick Street, New York, N. Y., offers a catalog which lists a number of paperback reprints of older books on gastronomical history.
• Gale Research has a large number of reprinted titles available.

Hot Lines

• Some cities have information "hot lines" that can be helpful since they allow you to work while somebody else does the looking up. If you live in Manhattan, try:
Library On Call: New York, 780-7817
Westchester, 914-682-8360

Special Libraries

• The Schlesinger Library
Radcliffe College
3 James Street
Radcliffe Yard
Cambridge, Mass.

This library houses six thousand cookbooks and related references. It answers "reasonable" questions by mail or phone (617-495-8647).

Government Pamphlets

• A wealth of material on cooking, health and nutrition is available free (or almost) from:
Consumer Information
Pueblo, Colorado 81009

Joining Up: Cooks and Writers Organizations
• You might benefit from joining a local writers' club and/or:
Women's National Book Association
P. O. Box 5024
FDR Station
New York, N. Y. 10022

(Write for address of the nearest chapter.)

• If you want to know more about the *only* national award competition honoring cookbook authors and their works (with a special award for the best "first" cookbook), write:

National Tastemaker Award Contest
c/o Harshe-Rotmen & Druck
300 East 44th Street
New York, N. Y. 10017

• Run a cooking school? Look into details on joining:

San Francisco Professional Food Society
c/o Anne Kupper, Williams Sonoma
5750 Hollis St.
Emeryville, Calif. 94608

Association of Cooking Schools
1001 Connecticut Ave. N.W.
Suite 800
Washington, D. C. 20036
(Enclose a stamped, self-addressed envelope).